MW00342756

Mathematics and Technology
in Elementary Education

First Edition

By Penina A. Kamina and Ray Siegrist

cognella® | ACADEMIC PUBLISHING

Bassim Hamadeh, CEO and Publisher
Kassie Graves, Director of Acquisitions
Jamie Giganti, Senior Managing Editor
Miguel Macias, Senior Graphic Designer
John Remington, Senior Field Acquisitions Editor
Monika Dziamka, Project Editor
Brian Fahey, Licensing Specialist
Rachel Singer, Associate Editor
Kat Ragudos, Interior Designer

Copyright © 2017 by Cognella, Inc. All rights reserved. No part of this publication may be reprinted, reproduced, transmitted, or utilized in any form or by any electronic, mechanical, or other means, now known or hereafter invented, including photocopying, microfilming, and recording, or in any information retrieval system without the written permission of Cognella, Inc.

Trademark Notice: Product or corporate names may be trademarks or registered trademarks, and are used only for identification and explanation without intent to infringe.

Cover image copyright © 2013 by iStockphoto LP / Christopher Futcher.

Printed in the United States of America

ISBN:978-1-63189-795-5 (pbk) / 978-1-63189-796-2 (br)

CONTENTS

ACKNOWLEDGMENTS

As mathematics educators, writing is not our forte, and we are truly grateful for those who gave their time to read the preliminary edition of our work. Thank you to the Fall 2015 teacher candidates of SUNY Oneonta in Blocks 25, 26, and 28 who looked at this work. We would also like to thank John Kamina, Monika Dziamka, and Rachel Singer for their valuable time spent reading the manuscript. Without your generosity, this work would mainly have been symbols and little to minimal text. Your efforts in reviewing this work has made it readily accessible without us relying wholly on mathematical signs and representations.

In general, teachers are teaching mathematics incorrectly by tackling only a small aspect of its understanding, despite the recommendations of research studies in mathematics education. The routine of presenting a problem and the way to solve the problem with plenty of practice leads to an emphasis on procedures at the expense of mathematical understanding. In such situations, when students are asked to explain their thinking, they use a procedure to explain their reasoning instead of a rationale of the concept.

Knowledge of procedures constitutes a small fraction of mathematical understanding, and as currently practiced is problematic. A lengthy review is required at the end of the year because students have forgotten which procedures go with certain problems. An alternate option to teaching mathematical procedure is to have the teacher shift authority. How?

A problem based on students' prior knowledge is posed. Students collaboratively attempt to solve the problem. If they cannot solve it, then the need to learn additional mathematics becomes apparent. Usually, a rich dialogue about mathematics is generated, assisted by the teacher. Students explain their solution or solution attempts, and finally they critique the mathematics of others. The two important points here are the need for learning new mathematics and the understanding required for explaining and critiquing. A procedure should not be accepted as an explanation.

Students need to be active in developing their understanding of mathematics. One way for students to be more responsible for their learning is to create a community of learning that incorporates activities and discussions that deepen students' understanding of mathematics. Attributes of a community of learning include inquiry, conjectures, self-correction, risk taking, appreciation of all contributions, vibrant dialogue, and much more.

Mathematics engages thinking that requires effort, but Kahneman (2011) writes that this thinking mechanism is lazy. For a teacher to get students to think requires determination because there is a natural resistance against the required effort. All students can learn mathematics if they expend effort. In the book *Mindset*, Dweck (2006) describes two types of mindsets: fixed and growth. A person with a fixed mindset believes you have it or you don't. The problem occurs when a fixed mindset person is presented with a problem he or she can't readily solve. Rather than take a risk, he or she states that the concept hasn't been learned yet. A lack of persistence in problem solving is evident. In a growth mindset, mistakes that are inevitable—as well as effort—are valued, thus encouraging people to improve. In fact, Moser, Schroder, Heeter, Moran, and

Lee (2011) concluded in a study that growth mindset people meet challenges better because they are on the lookout for mistakes.

Chialvo and Bak (1999) state that all learning occurs by making mistakes. Too often an opportunity is lost when a problem's solution is obtained. Most challenging problems generate interesting extensions along the solution path. In addition, students can ask what-if questions throughout the problem-solving process. In other words, the learning is not over when a solution is found. Students need to be responsible for their learning. If a student develops an algorithm to solve a problem, an understanding of the problem is exhibited. Dialogue ensues when the algorithm is explained and defended. In *Thinking Mathematically*, Mason, Burton, and Stacey (2010) encouraged the deepest scrutiny by telling students to convince an enemy (another student) that their thinking is sound.

In conclusion to this section, our teaching philosophy is grounded in constructivist and inquiry-based learning. We call on preservice teachers to try these approaches to their teaching and learning, to use a mindfulness approach in decision making, and most important of all, to consider student's learning as a first priority.

We merge both mathematics content knowledge and foundational pedagogical knowledge in this work. We also use research-based methods for teaching and learning of mathematics in the elementary classroom. The emphasis of our effort is on teaching mathematics for conceptual understanding as opposed to procedures, facts, applications, and skills only. The aim of teaching mathematics is for students to learn and know the concepts, which goes beyond solving given math problems correctly.

To be an effective mathematics teacher calls for not only professionalism but also the apt ability to plan each lesson well and to carry out its execution as well as reflection both in and on practice. We use the organization of a *lesson plan format* as the guiding framework in this book. A lesson plan is essential to instruction of mathematics since it documents how the *intended* curriculum is to be implemented and enacted. It is the puzzle piece and gist of instruction and thus is core to a teaching career. A lesson plan features what is taught in any given school day and is a building block of a unit, the learning segment of curriculum that takes 3 to 5 days to teach.

Globally, educators recognize the significance of a lesson plan. Rigelman (2011) notes that a "lesson is one piece of a broader mathematical storyline that builds over time" (p. 197). A lesson plan is the glue that holds the principles for school mathematics together. These principles for mathematics are curriculum, teaching, learning, assessment, equity, access, tools, and technology (Principles to Actions, 2014). Table 0.1 summarizes the link between key components of a lesson plan and core school mathematics principles.

Table 0.1: Lesson Plan Components Versus Principles

COMPONENTS OF LESSON PLAN	PRINCIPLES FOR SCHOOL MATHEMATICS
Big idea; central focus	Curriculum
Content and practice standards	Curriculum
Materials; resources	Tools
Prior/preassessment	Assessment
Instructional procedures: introduction, body, closure	Teaching and learning
Assessment: formative and/or summative	Assessment

(Continued)

COMPONENTS OF LESSON PLAN	PRINCIPLES FOR SCHOOL MATHEMATICS
Adaptations: differentiated instruction/accommodations/modifications	Access and equity
Technology connections	Technology
Extension activities; in-class enrichment; homework/practice task	Learning
Citation of lesson plan sources	Professionalism

In conclusion, it is important for teacher education programs to prepare mathematics teachers who can plan and teach effective lessons that incorporate both mathematics' content and its practices.

This book is for both the preservice and novice K–6 practicing teacher. The focal point is the knowledge and the skills they should have for the teaching and learning of mathematics as opposed to what their students learn in the classroom.

Pedagogy

Introduction

There are several courses a preservice teacher is expected to take before graduating to a teaching career. Preservice teachers must take classes from several departments, such as communication, arts and sciences, linguistics, sociology, philosophy, history, research and educational courses in psychology, curriculum studies, and didactics, as well as electives. A synthesis of ideas from these courses should empower a teacher candidate to have content knowledge, pedagogical knowledge, technological knowledge, and the ability to assess and evaluate students or programs, as well as develop appropriate professional dispositions and responsibilities. These are indispensable attributes for becoming an effective teacher who is proactive, is great at decision-making, and plans well.

Professionalism

There is no clear-cut definition of what professionalism is, but unspoken and a few written expectations are in place that varies from simple outward appearances to metacognition. Examples include the following:

- Modesty in dressing; no driving while impaired; no sexual harassment
- Positive disposition; cooperative; collaborative; punctual
- Up-to-date with current prevailing research findings or practices; active member of a professional organization
- Managerial skills—organized and has good management of time, classroom, records
- Reflective—on-the-spot reflection; reflection in action and reflection on action
- Noticing—attends, interprets, and responds (Jacob, Lamb, & Philipp, 2010)

Psychology

The theories learned from foundational education courses provide research-based reasons to ground and justify one's teaching practice. Table 1.1 gives a non-detailed sample of some theorists and their corresponding impact on instructional planning, teaching, and learning.

Table 1.1: Theory and Its Application

THEORIST	THEORY	EDUCATIONAL IMPLICATION
David Kolb (Learning)	Experiential learning that is motivating	Need for varied methods of teaching; multiple strategies and assessments
Erik Erikson (Psychosocial)	Life developmental stages	Group behaviors; personal identity; social identity
Jean Piaget (Cognitive)	Stages of cognitive development	Maturation; age-appropriate tasks and language use
Jean Lave and Etienne Wenger (Situated learning)	Communities of practice—social learning theory	Social norms of a classroom; knowledgeable; identity
Howard Gardner (Intelligence)	Multiple intelligences theory	Culturally responsive teaching; digital media; inculcation of students' interests
Lev Vygotsky (Social)	Social constructivism; zone of proximal development	Group work; peer scaffold; scaffold
Allan Paivio (Cognitive)	Dual coding	Representations; verbal; nonverbal
Jerome Bruner (Discovery)	Active learning; mental models	Hands-on activities; inquiry; exploration
Benjamin Bloom (Taxonomy of learning)	Learning domains—cognitive, affective, psychomotor, and levels	Classification of goals, learning objectives, questioning, and student behaviors; mastery learning

Pedagogy in General

Pedagogy, broadly defined, is all that pertains to the dynamics of teaching and learning—for example, techniques of instruction and approaches, motivation, curriculum, and assessment. Issues relating to being an effective teacher are applicable and pertinent to mathematics classrooms as well. It calls for the teacher's ability to do the following:

- Create a conducive learning environment and organize a classroom.
- Manage students, discipline, time, records of work, and instruction.
- Be well informed regarding the nature and scope of the content to teach.
- Integrate technology in teaching and learning.
- Motivate, respect, and create a positive rapport with students.
- Give clear directions to learning tasks.
- Actively engage the students in learning.
- Incorporate use of small group work, whole group work, and independent work.
- Include use of different representations, such as words, written text, visuals, and symbols.
- Offer adaptations, accommodations, modifications, and differentiated instruction and tasks by catering to all students—the above-target student, gifted and talented student, on-target student, below-target student, ESL student, and IEP student.
- Look into the best way to present the concept to a student meaningfully as well as in a culturally responsive way.

Is the teacher well versed in the merits and demerits of different approaches of teaching, such as scaffolding, case study, inquiry, lecture, discussion, programmed instruction, demonstration, discovery, project, questioning, multimedia case study, co-teaching, task analysis, educational trips, role-play, debate, problem-based, modeling, and so on. These approaches can be categorized as either teacher-centered or student-centered. Can the teacher effectively execute student-centered learning methods? Constructivism gives preference to the latter.

Using the questioning approach as an example, a teacher vested in constructivism should know that it is appropriate at any point in a lesson, and planning how to execute it well is needed. In planning, write a question for the introduction, the main body, and the closure of the lesson. Take into consideration the revised Bloom's taxonomy to come up with both low-order and high-order thinking questions. Teacher can pre-assess students by posing an opening question by writing it, displaying it, or projecting it to the class. Instead of a volunteer answering the question, the teacher can use the think-pair-share technique. During the lesson, the HRASE hierarchy can be employed. HRASE is a mnemonic for history, relationship, application, speculation, and explanation questioning technique. And finally, in closing the lesson, a 1-minute paper strategy can be applied; students can use an index card to write one thing they learned and one question they have about the lesson.

Ball, Thames, and Phelps (2008) came up with a framework for mathematical knowledge for teaching that encompasses overlaps of pedagogy, curriculum content, and students, with special reference to mathematics.

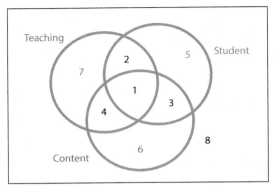

Figure 1.1: Intersectional Ties of Educational Knowledge

They have defined their six areas in their article in depth, using examples and counterexamples. Their work informs our discussion of Figure 1.1.

If we look at the rectangle in Figure 1.1, it represents the universal set, which in this case is the varied type of educational knowledge that impacts the teaching career. Examples of what falls in the portion numbered 8 are knowledge of educational law or knowledge of curriculum. Broadly, a teacher candidate should have knowledge of curriculum, such as: Where does curriculum come from? Who writes curriculum? What is the difference between intended and enacted or implemented curriculum? What is spiral or hierarchical curriculum? What does knowledge of vertical and horizontal curriculum entail in a specified content area?

The portion numbered 1 and 3 on Figure 1.1 is the overlap of two types of knowledge— the subject-specific content and knowledge of students. This knowledge enables a teacher to weigh in and make appropriate decisions. For example, if first-grade students were asked to find the difference between 16 and 5, some students may state that 16 has two digits and 5 has one digit, instead of subtracting 5 from 16. Thus, a teacher knowing that students may have encountered the term *difference* in other experiences uses that to distinguish the meaning as used in everyday language versus how it is used in the operation of subtraction. The teacher should be prepared to deal with arising misconceptions, errors, misunderstandings, and partial understandings and should know how to enrich teaching and learning.

On the other hand, the area labeled 1 and 4 on Figure 1.1, the intersection of content knowledge and knowledge of teaching, empowers a teacher to weigh in a different way from number 3. For instance, this knowledge helps a teacher structure instruction by selecting "which examples to start with and which examples to use to take students deeper into the content" (Ball et al., 2008, p. 401). Another example is the ability of a teacher to pick out appropriate materials and resources for a given lesson, like using pattern blocks for teaching benchmark fractions such as halves, thirds, and sixths, since the blocks lend themselves to such content. Thus, in teaching fourths, fifths, and sevenths, a different manipulative would suffice.

To be properly situated in teaching mathematics effectively, the teacher candidates must be knowledgeable in mathematics content—areas 1, 3, 4, and 6 of Figure 1.1. The teacher should know the ins and outs of what is required for students to learn.

In conclusion to Section 1, a well-grounded teacher candidate should be able to easily transfer these varied learning theories and pedagogies in any given learning context. So when it comes to teaching in a mathematics classroom, he or she should pinpoint what specific mathematics moves there are in the K–6 classrooms. What does questioning, discussion, demonstration, inquiry-based learning, problem-based learning, or differentiated instructional technique look like in K–6 mathematics classrooms?

TERMS TO PONDER		
Modeling	Inquiry-based learning	Investigation
Problem-based learning	Experiment	Scaffolding
HRASE technique	Discussion	Discourse
Games	Questioning	Math workshop
Collaborative groups	Interview	Math stations

ACTIVITY 1.1: Carry out research on one 21st-century educational theorist (behaviorist, developmental psychologist, cognitive scientist, sociocultural theorist, motivational psychologist, educational philosopher, learning theorist, and so on). Who is he or she? What approach is taken? What is the principle of the theory or research? What does he or she talk about? What is the connection of his or her work to the elementary child? What is the impact of the theory or research on K–6 teaching and learning? What does this mean to you?

ACTIVITY 1.2: Draw a number line on teaching approaches and label one end "Teacher Centered" and the other "Student Centered." Write down all the teaching approaches you know on this continuum.

ACTIVITY 1.3: Why is it important to use methods that actively involve students? Justify using these specific techniques: (a) discussion, (b) Q & A, and (c) 1-minute paper.

ACTIVITY 1.4: Several questions are posed in Section 1. Some of these questions are answered in upcoming pages of this book. Can you find them as you read the text?

Websites

www.amte.net   *Teachers:* The Association of Mathematics Teacher Educators (AMTE) is the largest professional organization in the nation devoted to the improvement of mathematics teacher education by supporting the preservice education and professional development of K–12 teachers of mathematics. The AMTE provides dates for conferences, various publications, research information, resources for teachers, and news concerning the field of mathematics education.

www.todos-math.org *Teachers*: This is a website for TODOS, is an organization that supports mathematics for all students—in particular, Latina/o students. This website provides information on promoting equity and high-quality math education for all students through professional development.

www.bannekermath.org *Teachers:* The Benjamin Banneker Association is a national nonprofit organization dedicated to mathematics education advocacy, leadership, and professional development. The site provides information on workshops, publications, various awards and recognitions, and additional news and resources in order to support teachers in leveling the playing field for mathematics learning of the highest quality for African American students.

www.T2T-I.org *Teachers*: Teachers2Teachers International provides ongoing professional development and resources to influential, high-impact teachers in selected schools around the world. This program connects classroom teachers with experienced teacher–coaches, emphasizing a culturally sensitive approach that encourages student-centered instruction using community-learning goals.

www.mentoringminds.com *Teachers*: Mentoring Minds is a national educational publisher developing proven K–12 instructional materials that encourage critical thinking for life. Mentoring Minds aims to motivate children to think critically and to learn effective problem-solving skills in the classroom, which will increase their chances for success and prepare them for life in the 21st-century global marketplace. Product subjects include math, reading, writing, vocabulary, Spanish, and science. Product materials include assessments, classroom management tips, and guide to critical thinking, flip charts, online solutions, and wheels.

https://uteach.utexas.edu *Teachers:* UTeach aims to prepare mathematics and science teachers for the field of education. UTeach also provides professional development for teachers currently working in K–12 settings. There are summer academies, after-school workshops, and various other professional development opportunities available.

www.toolsofthemind.org *Teachers:* Tools of the Mind is a research-based program combining early childhood pedagogy with an innovative curriculum that helps young children develop the cognitive, social–emotional, self-regulatory, and foundational academic skills they need to succeed in school and beyond. Currently, Tools of the Mind has two complementary modules: one designed to be used with children aged 3 to 4 in pre-K and preschool settings, and the other designed for kindergarten. Knowledge of technology, engineering, or math and empowers students the opportunity to expand their knowledge in the area of their choosing.

Mathematical Pedagogy

Introduction

Instruction of mathematics requires much more than is discussed in this section. Topics like professionalism, responsibilities, and discussion that were covered in Section 1 are assumed to be in place. In teaching mathematics effectively, the teacher candidates must be knowledgeable in mathematics content and practices in order to be able to guide students and facilitate their learning of mathematics. In this section we look at mathematical moves, mathematical knowledge for teaching, and mathematical understandings.

Mathematical Moves

Teaching and learning in any mathematics classroom should integrate best practices by observing specific psychological considerations, displaying sound epistemology, and incorporating relevant instructional methods and moves. Such best practices also focus on technology, emphasize assessment, align with Common Core State Standards for Mathematics (CCSSM), and establish safe learning environment with suitable sociomathematical norms.

Research in mathematics education favors teaching progressively from concrete to semiconcrete to abstraction and the use of constructivist approaches in the mathematics classroom. The teachers should encourage students to construct knowledge by providing hands-on learning and problem-solving opportunities and by allowing discourse in the classroom.

As a teacher candidate, facilitating teaching and learning of mathematics calls for use of methods, strategies, and techniques or *moves* that are student centered, allowing students to participate and be actively involved. Some commonly used moves are discussed, and they may overlap each other.

Talk move is useful in the *main body* of a mathematics lesson. In discussion, pose questions to students to probe, clarify, or verify and provide necessary support. Talk move is using students' thinking to enhance reasoning skills. In sharing solutions after solving a problem, students can discuss how logical, valid, and reasonable the offered answer is. "Key components of this discussion are the specific instructional actions ... prompting students to consider whether more than one answer could be correct, to identify reasonable solutions, to offer counterexamples, and to compare the efficiency of strategies" (Gengiz, 2013, p. 450). An explicit, clear, and open-ended question enhances rich discussion, which in turn opens the door to students' thinking, permitting a teacher to extend these thoughts.

Student thinking move is the constructive incorporation of student thinking into teaching and learning. This moves demands a *teacher noticing move* that involves attention, analysis, interpretation, and response to students' mathematical thinking. The teacher must track, build, and focus on student knowledge construction.

Questioning move can be used appropriately anytime in a lesson and should contain both low- and high-level probes, which can be easily planned for based on the revised Bloom's taxonomy. There are many techniques that can greatly enhance the *questioning move*, such as the think-pair-share strategy, turn and talk, cueing, *show me*, one-on-one, and so on.

Assessment moves also exist. *One-minute paper* can be used in the introduction, to summarize a previously assigned work, or in the closure of a lesson. Other ways to assess students in any part of the lesson—be it the introduction, main body, or closure—are *poll everywhere, focused listing,* and *compare answer* technique.

Use of example move is vital in teaching mathematics because it causes a shift in conceptualization and serves different purposes, such as exemplification, concept definition, and visualization of a concept. Productive use of example entails offering varied types of examples, such as nonexample, counterexample, connections, similarities, and differences.

Practice move enables students to master and exercise a learned skill, algorithm, rule, or procedure. The format of practice could be a written worksheet, a game, drill-and-practice software, a quiz, or a song.

Demonstration move (scaffold) is teacher based at first, with a gradual release of responsibility to students. The strategy of *I do—we do—you do* is often employed. In it, the teacher explains how to solve a problem to the whole class. Next, the whole class chimes in to solve a second question of the same skill as the first one, and finally each student independently solves a third question using a similar step-by-step method as that demonstrated. A variation of this could be *we do—pairs do—you do.*

Interaction move deals with how classroom collaboration is facilitated and comprises whole class work, small group work, partner work, and independent work. For example, in individual work, a teacher may require a student to explain the reasoning of a solution path. It is paramount that a teacher strategizes ways to transition from one form of interaction to another, be it teacher–whole class or student–student or student–whole class or teacher–student.

"I can" move is a learning target and is a statement for students; for example, "I am able to use the near doubles facts two add two consecutive numbers." The teacher should write learning targets, ask the class to read and discuss with a partner the relevance, and have students self-assess to monitor their own progress. This approach gives student a voice and allows student to take responsibility for his or her own learning. The teacher needs to facilitate ways for the students to restate lesson objective their own words and to self-assess with regard to the learning target.

Mathematical Knowledge for Teaching

Specialized content knowledge (SCK), which is one of the domains of mathematical knowledge for teaching (Ball Thames & Phelps, 2008), is of utmost importance to teacher candidates. SCK is the "skill unique to teaching ... knowledge not typically needed for purposes other than teaching" (Ball et al., 2008, p. 400). For example, in teaching whole number subtraction, a teacher candidate should consider use of authentic real-world problems that permit use of different thinking approaches or representations:

- *Tim has 6 seedlings, but 2 of them wilted. How many are live?* This is an example of the *take away* approach using a *set model*, where you take away some objects from a set of objects.
    - ◊ A set model is an object or a representation that is countable, such as paperclips, chairs, and students in a class.
- *Kim has 6 feet of ribbon. She uses 2 feet of ribbon to wrap a gift. How much ribbon is left?* This is an example of the *take away* approach using the *measurement model*, where you take away a certain measure from a given measure.
    - ◊ Measurement models are objects or representations that are uncountable but can be measured, such as height and temperature.
- *Sammy has 6 cuddly bears, while Mutts has 2. How many more bears does Sammy have than Mutts?* This is an example of the *comparison approach* using a *set model*, where you find how many more objects one set has than another.
- *Dottie needs to save 6 dollars for a concert. So far she has 2 dollars. How much more does she still need?* This is an example of the *missing addend* approach using a *set model*, where you find what you need to add to the given addend to make the total amount.

These four bulleted questions are subtraction problems of whole numbers—if decontextualized, they give $6 - 2 = ?$ as the number sentence.

The number sentence $6 - 2 = 4$ is abstract, uses symbols, aids in procedural fluency, and is very easy to memorize, but rote learning does not enable a student to make sense of the contextualized problems; therefore, both the context and the equation are important to know. A teacher should first teach meaningfully before moving to procedures. The use of context supports students in comprehending the meaning of subtraction, after which the equation can be introduced for students to reason abstractly and quantitatively and to attend to precision.

Another illustration of possessing SCK is the ability to teach whole number division that incorporates varied approaches of thinking:

- *We have 12 mangoes for 4 of us. How many will each person get if we share equally?* This is an example of *partitive division* using a set model, where there are a fixed number of groups and you *share* the objects equally in each group to determine the size of a group.
- *A walking competition is 12 kilometers long. How long will it take Sarah to finish if she averages 4 kilometers per hour?* This is an example of *measurement division*, and it involves *repeated subtraction* of equal sizes to determine how many groups of these you get.
- *John has a dozen eggs. How many 4-egg omelets can he make?* This is an example of *measurement division* using a set model.

Again, these three bulleted questions deal with the concept of division of whole numbers, and when decontextualized each is written as a number sentence: $12 \div 4 = ?$ The use of equations alone does not feature the thinking approaches and models embedded in the operation of division. The teacher should consider giving varied learning tasks that explore different thinking approaches.

The use of equations in division can be used to rewrite a division number sentence, $12 \div 4 = ?$, as a multiplication sentence: $4 \times ? = 12$; there is a factor required to balance the equation. This way of thinking about the concept of division is referred to as the *missing-factor* approach.

Mathematical Understandings

Mathematics instruction requires comprehension and familiarity with what *mathematical understandings* are. They include conceptual understanding, procedural fluency, mathematical reasoning, and problem solving. What does each mean? The importance of comprehending the terms, *conceptual understanding, procedural fluency, mathematical reasoning,* and *problem solving* is vital to teaching and learning mathematics. Teachers need to balance the practice of each, as opposed to overemphasizing one over the rest.

For years now, the practice of diminishing mathematical understandings to solving routine problems by following rules blindly is a well-known fact that should not be perpetuated in the 21st-century framework.

Conceptual Understanding

Conceptual understanding deals with understanding the meaning of mathematical concepts and their relationships. Examples of a student with conceptual understanding include the following:

- Has the ability to write quantities in more than one way; for example, 4, four, ////, $40 - 36$, $3 + 8 - 7$.
- Defines *addition* as putting together like objects; for example, it is not possible to add $\frac{1}{2}$ to $\frac{1}{4}$ because a half and a fourth are not alike and the only way would be to divide the half into fourths. Therefore, one half becomes two fourths, making them alike: $\frac{1}{2} + \frac{1}{4} = \frac{2}{4} + \frac{1}{4} = \frac{3}{4}$.
- Applies thinking strategies such as combinations of tens, properties of operations, doubles and near doubles, fact families, skip counting, and equal addends to find the solution to problems.
- Has the ability to compare, contrast, and integrate related concepts and principles.
- Comprehends and uses mathematical notations like 0, $\frac{1}{2}$, $+$, $=$, %, $>$, 37, 6^0, 45km, $3x + 4$, -22, and vocabulary such as products, volume, expressions, equivalence, power, dividend, minuend, and so on.
- Has understanding of math concepts like place value—the position of a number indicates its value with reference to the ones; for example, 7 tens is actually 70 ones when unbundled, or 87 ones is 8 tens and 7 ones when bundled. Such a student appreciates the conciseness of place value notions.

Conceptual understanding is synonymous with Skemp's (1976) *relational understanding*, which is the knowledge that helps in reconstruction of forgotten facts and techniques and involves making sense of concepts. Skemp encourages teaching rules, algorithms, and procedures after students have discovered the relationships of the mathematical concepts.

EXAMPLE: *Solving* $\frac{1}{2} \times \frac{3}{4}$ *conceptually*

To determine the value of $\frac{1}{2} \times \frac{3}{4}$ requires finding three fourths of one half or vice versa. An area model can be used to find the solution to multiplication of a fraction by a fraction.

Start with the whole shape and find half of it.

The shaded portion is half of the whole shape:

Divide the shaded portion into four equal parts. Note that in so doing, the whole shape is now divided into eight equal parts:

Consider three parts of shaded portions.

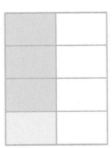

The darker shaded portion is three fourths of one half, which is three eighths of the whole shape. Therefore, $\frac{1}{2} \times \frac{3}{4} = \frac{3}{8}$.

Alternatively, by reasoning, you can determine $\frac{1}{2}$ of $\frac{3}{4}$, or $\frac{3}{4}$ of $\frac{1}{2}$. The operation of "of" means "×" (multiply) and is of a higher hierarchy in the order of mathematical conventions of operations.

Procedural Fluency

Procedural fluency deals with a step-by-step process of solving mathematical problems, such as seen with the standard vertical algorithm of addition and subtraction, long multiplication, or long division. It refers to knowledge of the what, when, and how of a procedure or a rule or algorithm. According to *Adding It Up* (National Research Council, 2001), procedural fluency is a skill in performing "procedures flexibly, accurately, efficiently and appropriately" and is identical to Skemp's (2006) instrumental understanding, which he states are "rules without reasons" (p. 89) The caution for teacher candidates is to teach a math concept meaningfully first before venturing into its procedure.

We will use the concept of perimeter to explain. Given that *perimeter* is a vocabulary for primary elementary students, there is need for a definition followed by an example using a benchmark shape such as rectangle and also stating a counterexample. Next, engage students in finding the perimeter of different rectangles they can form using 12 colored tiles by counting the distance (unit lengths) around it, with emphasis on the starting point and the end point being the same.

Three different rectangles can be formed. A rectangle measuring 12 by 1 will have a perimeter of 26 units; a 4 by 3 will have 14 units, and a 6 by 2 will have 16 units. A task like this supports conceptual understanding of perimeter. But equally important is the ability to be efficient. So wean students off the color tiles, which is a hands-on task that involves use of concrete objects, by drawing and labeling a rectangle, a semiconcrete representation, and then setting up an equation, $12 + 1 + 12 + 1 = 26$, a symbolic representation. Students with competency in multiplication should simplify it as $2(12) + 2(1) = 26$ and use algebraic thinking to generalize for any rectangle, $P = 2W + 2L$, to show abstraction in their thinking.

The use of a formula and simply substituting ("plugging in") the numbers enables students to find perimeter quickly in an efficient and accurate manner. Additionally, once the formula is understood, build students' knowledge of the relationship between P, W, and L. If the values of any two of these are known, can they determine the third missing value; for example, if the perimeter is 26cm and length is 12cm, can the width be found?

Merriam-Webster's dictionary defines the word *fluent* as "done in a smooth and easy way." To achieve fluency with a procedure, it must have flexible, efficient, and appropriate attributes, with the end result of giving an accurate solution. The use of the formula for finding perimeter of a rectangle, $P = 2(L + W)$, alone is a procedure. There is need for the procedure to be *efficient*, be a shortcut, or save time for fluency. Fluency in a procedure requires automaticity and keenness.

A procedure should be *appropriate*. For example, in simplifying a fraction, students like to cancel common factors, allowing for one to fluently leave the answer in its simplest form, such as $\frac{3xy}{y} = \frac{3x}{1}$, which is good, but performing the same procedure on a problem like $\frac{sinx}{x} \neq \frac{sin}{1}$ is *inappropriate*. A procedure for algebraic functions does not necessarily work for trigonometric functions. Similarly, the use of distributivity in expansion of an expression is at times overgeneralized from one function to another; for example, $x(6 + y) = 6x + xy$, but $\cos(x + 30^0) \neq \cos x + \cos 30^0$.

Why is there such over-transference of a procedure? Do students realize that what works for one function may not hold true for another function?

Again, there is need to be *flexible* in choosing an appropriate procedure to apply in order to be to be fluent; for example, in simplifying $6 + 7$, using "near doubles" is the best thinking strategy, while doing so for $6 + 9$ is not. Using "combinations of ten" would be the best thinking strategy for simplifying $6 + 9$.

Likewise, flexibility is needed in rewriting a procedure backward in order to be fluent and accurate. In teaching procedures, provide a variety of examples under which the algorithm works; besides modeling how to use *invert and multiply* in a problem such as

$$5 \div \frac{1}{4}, \text{ also give } \frac{1}{4} \div 5.$$

Most students who know the first one only will memorize the steps of the invert-and-multiply procedure and may have difficulty rewriting the second one, $\frac{1}{4} \div 5$, because in their mind the whole number is transposed incorrectly. In short, ensure you vary the dividends and divisors; have some divisors that are fractions and some that are whole numbers. Also, consider unit fractions versus nonunit fractions and do so, too, with the dividend:

- $9 \div \frac{4}{5}$

- $\frac{1}{5} \div \frac{1}{6}$

- $\frac{2}{3} \div 8$

- $1\frac{3}{4} \div 2$

- $1\frac{3}{4} \div \frac{1}{2}$

Review the invert-and-multiply procedure again for all these options to look for, and express regularity in repeated reasoning (Standard for Mathematical Practices).

Note that there are several algorithms that students need to know, and there is still a need to comprehend why it works in the given situation. Again, teach a math concept meaningfully first before venturing into its procedure(s), and if necessary remember to delineate the set of numbers and the boundaries for which the procedure works.

EXAMPLE: *Solving* $\frac{1}{2} \times \frac{3}{4}$ *procedurally*

$$\frac{\text{Numerator} \times \text{Numerator}}{\text{Denominator} \times \text{Denominator}} = \frac{1}{2} \times \frac{3}{4} = \frac{1 \times 3}{2 \times 4} = \frac{3}{8}$$

Problem Solving

Problem-solving techniques provide skills to participate "in a task for which the solution method is not known in advance" (Principles and Standards for School Mathematics, 2000, p. 52). The CCSSM's (2010) first standard for mathematical practice is "make sense of problems" and not only that, but to "persevere in solving them." Reys, Lindquist, Lambdin, & Smith (2012) are in agreement that problem solving encourages sense making in *nonroutine problems*—which they define as a situation in which the solution route is not immediately obvious. A counterexample to problem solving is an *exercise*, a situation in which the solution route is obvious and whose purpose is drill and practice to develop fluency, or a *routine problem*—the application of a mathematical procedure in the same way it was learned (Reys et. al, 2012).

> *Write a word problem for which 25kg 32g – 23kg 83g =* _____ *would be the solution equation.*
> (Retrieved on August 2014 from https://www.EngageNY.org grade 4, module 2, question 3b of the end-of-module assessment)
> calls for problem solving skills.)

Solving the given equation to obtain 1,949g, or 1kg 949g, is an exercise, since fourth graders have had plenty of practice subtracting mixed masses but not in writing a word problem, making this a problem-solving task.

We believe a fourth grader may ask, "What is a word problem? What should I do here?" Once a student understands what a word problem is, the next difficulty to anticipate is that the context of the student's word problem may not align with mass (kg). For example, a student may ignore the units involved and write, "Tanya rode her bike for 25kg 32g, and Tony rode his bike for 23kg 83g. How much farther did Tanya ride than Tony?" A student may forget that the units, kg or g, measure mass and not distance.

Problem solving allows students to use critical thinking and varied prior knowledge to solve a given task. Students engage in the problem-solving process when there is no apparent path to the problem's solution. They need to be explicitly taught a general problem-solving strategy. Using a KWL chart will help students organize what they are doing while problem solving. Also, cooperative problem solving allows students to refine their thoughts through dialogue.

The first step in the strategy should be to understand the problem. Students often have difficulty in beginning the solution process because they do not understand what they are reading. Developing literacy is an important foundation. A way to assess students' understanding is to look at what they have written in the "Know" part of their chart.

Frustration is a part of the problem-solving process. If a student becomes frustrated, feedback is the answer. Feedback does not entail giving students the answer or telling students how to solve the problem, because this does not help develop problem-solving skills. A good start is to have the student explain what she or he is doing and why. Straightening out misconceptions is one role the teacher assumes. The goal is to solve the problem (the larger goal is for the students to become independent problem solvers). The student is on the path to achieving the goal; feedback explains how the student goes from where she or he is to the goal. The teacher helps create a plan with the student.

A good strategy is for each student to have a problem-solving folder that can be considered a portfolio. Students can put an unfinished problem in their folder and come back to it at a later time to eliminate overwhelming frustration. Not giving up develops perseverance. Students can also use their folders to observe their progress over time in developing their problem-solving skills.

Differentiation can easily be implemented—for example, by assigning easier problems to struggling students, providing more time to complete problems, or pairing struggling and nonstruggling students. Keep the groups fluid; in other words, don't expect the same students to remain in the struggling group. Formative assessment is key.

Pictures are a very good way for students to organize their thoughts and knowledge. Labeling pictures and values is an important skill for students to develop. The next step is to make a plan for solving the problem. This step prevents students from randomly trying procedures and operations. The "What" part of the KWL chart should contain the problem-solving plan. Alternate plans can be noted in case the selected one does not work out.

While problem solving, students need to continually ask themselves whether what they are doing is helping them achieve the solution. Are the results reasonable? Also, have they seen any previous problems that are like this problem? As they solve problems, can they add information to the "Know" part of their plans that will help in the problems' solutions?

The final part of the process is to fill out the "Learned" part of their chart. Did she or he use a previously learned process to solve the problem? Can an inference be made about this specific problem that will help solve this type of problem? Were any mathematical operations, processes, or concepts seen from a different viewpoint?

Mathematical Reasoning

Mathematical reasoning varies from one task to the other, with the end result of using valid logic correctly. For example, a primary student who has a quarter may be very happy to trade it for four nickels. The logic used by this young student of "FOUR things ($0.05) is more than ONE thing ($0.25) and thus better" is correct but invalid.

In mathematical reasoning, students are expected to make sense of their solutions by explaining or justifying the steps taken and reflecting on the rationale of doing so. Checking the reasonableness of answers is significant, as is making conjectures. The students' sense making can be written or verbalized either as a whole class or in small groups.

Mathematical reasoning is usually a key component in mathematical discussions. Also, its significance is evidenced by 50% of the CCSSM standards for mathematical practice, namely:

- Reason abstractly and quantitatively
- Construct viable arguments and critique the reasoning of others
- Look for and make use of structure
- Look for and express regularity in repeated reasoning

Look for and make use of structure is inductive reasoning (bottom-up logic). It is a scenario where one looks for similar instances and then makes a generalization.

Primary students can notice that $2 + 0 = 2$, and in another instance $0 + 9 = 9$, and in a third instance $10 + 0 = 10$. From more instances, they begin to conjecture that a number added to zero stays the same. The class may then generalize that adding zero to any number leaves it unchanged.

On the other hand, *look for and express regularity in repeated reasoning* is deductive (top-down logic) reasoning. One has a broader picture, a generalization, and works with instances; for example, the generalization can be "angle sum of a triangle is 180 degrees." Examples of different instances based on this generalization can be:

- A triangle can only have one 90^0 angle
- An isosceles triangle is an acute triangle
- A triangle can only have one obtuse angle
- If all the lengths of a triangle are equal, then so are the angles, which equal 60^0

An example of a simple activity for mathematical reasoning that upper elementary students can engage in is to find the angle sum of a triangle.

1. Students draw different types of triangles.
2. Measure each of the three openings with a protractor.
3. Find the sum of these measures.
4. After many more of these instances, they should make conjectures. Students should reach the conclusion that whether the triangle is isosceles, equilateral, right angled, scalene, acute, or obtuse, the angle sum is the same.
5. Finally, students should generalize that the angle sum of a triangle is 180^0.

In conclusion to this section, teaching and learning of mathematics require foundational pedagogy, pedagogical knowledge pertinent to mathematics, knowledge of mathematics content, and well-balanced mathematical understandings.

TERMS TO PONDER		
Specialized content knowledge	"I can" statement	Low-risk environment
Abstract	Symbolic	Semiconcrete
Problem solving	Differentiate	Conceptual understanding
Mathematical reasoning	Procedural fluency	Teacher noticing
Metacognitive awareness	Small groups	Making connections
Computational fluency	Visuals	Cueing
Algorithm	Use tools strategically	Turn and talk

ACTIVITY 2.1: Use the missing-factor approach to solve the following:

$12 \div 0 = ?$

$84 \div 7 = ?$

$0 \div 4 = ?$

$3 \div 51 = ?$

ACTIVITY 2.2: Use an area model to show (a) $\frac{1}{2}$ of 4 and (b) 4 of $\frac{1}{2}$.

ACTIVITY 2.3: Write an assessment of not more than four questions based on any K–6 CCSSM standard that targets conceptual understanding, procedural fluency, problem solving, and mathematical reasoning.

ACTIVITY 2.4: (a) Solve the problem in Figure 2.1.

The Smith family is fund-raising to donate to the Red Cross by selling bags of rice in the market this weekend. They have 37kg to pack in bags that hold 3kg each. The 4 neighbors heard about their project and each gave 5kg to the Smiths; another family, the Hernandezes, also brought 11kg of rice to the Smiths.

(a) Write an equation using the letter x to find the number of bags to pack all the rice available.

$$x = \underline{\hspace{5cm}}$$

(b) How many bags are needed to pack the rice if each bag weighs 3kg? Explain.

(c) If a bag is sold for $4.50, how much is raised if all the rice is sold? Show your work.

(b) Fill in the graphic organizer to explicitly list all the specific math concepts, facts, procedures, problem-solving skills, and reasoning skills embedded in the assessment questions in Figure 2.1.

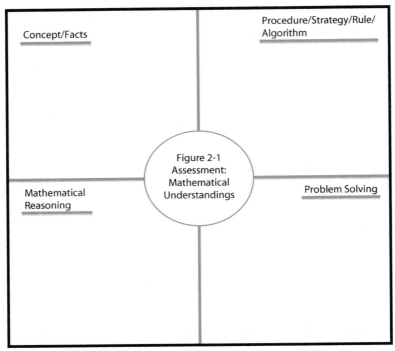

Figure 2.1: Operation and Algebraic Thinking

www.mathforum.org/NCTM   *Teachers:* This website provides teachers with information concerning a variety of topics in the field of education. The website is hosted by Drexel University of Education and presents its visitors with forums on mathematics learning and teaching.

www.youcubed.org   *Teachers:* This website can be used by administrators, teachers, and parents for up-to-date information on mathematics education. YouCubed is a nonprofit providing free and affordable K–12 mathematics resources and professional development for educators and parents.

www.mathsolutions.com

Teachers: Math Solutions is a website dedicated to improving students' learning of mathematics by providing educators with the highest quality professional development services and resources. Math Solutions works with schools to help better math instruction for all students. A variety of books, resources, and Common Core support are provided to help schools succeed in developing effective math instruction.

www.actuarialfoundation.org

Teachers: The Actuarial Foundation is an organization established to help facilitate and broaden the profession's contribution to society. The foundation explores innovative ways to apply actuarial skills (financial impact of risk and uncertainty) in the public interest. This website has information on sponsorships, scholarships, research, events, and programs.

www.IXL.com

Tools/Teachers: This website provides examples of math problems that teachers can give to their students for practice. The websites covers pre-K through high school and includes categories for all the topics covered in each grade. Teachers can also choose what topics they study based on their state and standards.

www.commoncore.org (Eureka math)

Teachers: This is a website for Eureka Math, which follows the Common Core State Standard curriculum for grades pre-K through 12.

www.learner.org

Teachers/Tools: This website shares teacher resources and professional development for teachers across the curriculum. The goal of Annenberg Learner is to improve the overall quality of education in America. This website includes professional development opportunities, lesson plans, interactive tools, and blogs.

Pre-K–6 Mathematics Curriculum

Introduction

In this section, we look at specific ways of teaching and learning mathematics. We discuss teaching and learning of the K–6 mathematics curriculum with special references to the following:

  (i) New York State P–12 Common Core Learning Standards for Mathematics (NYCCLS-M), which includes the entire CCSSM plus other mathematics standards needed in New York, such as ordinal numbers, tell and write money, and so forth

 (ii) Eureka Math (http://commoncore.org/maps/math/home)

(iii) EngageNY (https://www.engageny.org/common-core-curriculum)

In this section, we use abbreviations heavily to draw attention to *content* and *practice* standards embedded in K–6 mathematics curriculum. For instance, the term *practice* connotes many meanings in common language usage (exercise, tradition), which is different from how it is used in the K–6 mathematics curriculum; thus our preference for *SMP* to make it stand out.

Curriculum

Currently several US States are using the Common Core mathematics or CCSSM. It has two types of standards; that is, the mathematical content standards and mathematical practice standards. The K–6 math standards are briefly investigated here: What are they, and what implications do they have for teaching and learning mathematics?

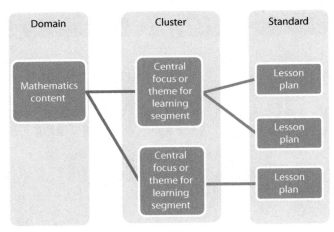

Figure 3.1: From Intended to Enacted Curriculum

The terms *domain*, *cluster*, and *standard* are used in CCSSM to break down mathematics content goals into daily or weekly teachable portions, in a conical model, as shown in Figure 3.1.

A lesson plan must have an objective(s) derived from NYCCLS-M standards. The standards included in a lesson plan should encompass both the mathematics *content* standard(s) and standard(s) for mathematical practice (SMP). These two standards are integrated during instruction. One should not plan to teach an SMP without a math content.

K-6 Mathematical Content Standards

CCSSM does not have math standards for prekindergarten, but the NYCCLS-M's curriculum does. Both their mathematical *content* standards comprise ten domains. These are:

Counting and Cardinality—CC

Number and Operations in Base Ten—NBT

Numbers and Operations-Fractions—NF

Operations and Algebraic Thinking—OA

Measurement and Data—MD

Geometry—G

Expressions and Equations—EE

Statistics and Probability—SP

Ratios and Proportional Relationships—RP

The Number System—NS

The domains taught in each of the elementary classrooms are listed in Table 3.1. It shows the grade level where each domain is introduced and where its coverage ends. The math concepts covered in the domains are arranged in a developmentally age-appropriate sequence and follow both a hierarchical and a spiral curriculum.

In Table 3.1 note that the majority of the topics in K–6 curriculum have a heavy focus on *number sense and operations*, one of the National Council of Teachers of Mathematics' (NCTM) major branches of mathematics. These are CC, OA, NBT, NF, RP, and NS.

Likewise the OA, NBT, MD, and G are taught annually from prekindergarten to fifth grade. Despite the domain being the same, there is a variation in the complexity of the concept as students move up a grade. As pointed out by psychologist Jerome Bruner, this is the *spiral* nature of mathematics curriculum,

Table 3.1: K–6 Distribution of Domains

K	1	2	3	4	5	6
CC						
OA	OA	OA	OA	OA	OA	
NBT	NBT	NBT	NBT	NBT	NBT	
MD	MD	MD	MD	MD	MD	
G	G	G	G	G	G	G
			NF	NF	NF	RP
						NS
						EE
						SP

where a math concept is reviewed again and deepened at a higher grade level, surpassing the previous concept coverage. Additionally, the content standards in second-grade OA are different from third-grade OA, but they build on each other, which is the *hierarchical* nature of mathematics curriculum. It pinpoints prerequisite or prior knowledge and what to pre-assess before launching new concepts; that is, 2.OA.4 is a prerequisite for 3.OA.1.

The fact that mathematics content curriculum is both hierarchical and spiral in nature, has implications for its teaching and learning. Thus, in lesson planning, besides a aligning the instructional objectives to a content standard, teachers should put effort into incorporating either vertical or horizontal math curriculum. What is vertical or horizontal math curriculum?

Typically, *vertical* suggests going "up and down," so this is viewing the targeted math content standard in relation to the standard below it and the one above it. Broadly, a second-grade math teacher should also focus on the same mathematical domain at the first and third levels. Possessing a vertical curriculum perception delineates the boundaries of the math content. Moreover, it shows how much content to include that is developmentally appropriate to students. Generally, vertical curriculum is crucial in teaching in several dimensions. Teaching a certain age group or grade calls for knowing curriculum below as well as the above this group or grade. For example, a sixth-grade teacher should be conversant with the fifth- and seventh-grade curriculum. In addition, in teaching a targeted concept, both prior knowledge and knowing the next steps are crucial.

On the other hand, *horizontal* implies going "across." Thus, teaching and learning a targeted math content standard calls for looking into its connection within mathematics itself and within other school subjects, as well as its application to real-world problems. Having a horizontal curriculum view grounds the math concept and makes teaching and learning meaningful.

The teaching and learning of pre-K–6 mathematics concepts moves from concrete to semiconcrete to abstract. This progression is affiliated with Bruner's developmental learning and proceeds from enactive stage to iconic stage and finally to symbolic stage.

The CCSSM math content standards at prekindergarten to grade 2, the primary elementary level, has more enactive learning, more play, lots of hands-on activities, some iconic, and less symbolism. At the intermediate level, grades 3 to 4, there are some enactive learning, more iconic, and some symbolism. At the upper elementary level, grades 5 to 6, there is less enactive learning, some iconic, and more symbolism. Although hands-on learning or use of manipulatives at the introductory level of a concept is crucial in laying a firm foundation, so is the weaning that leads to abstraction. This trend can be seen in Table 3.2 on the pre-K–6 geometry topic.

Table 3.2: Central Focus of Geometry Domain From Pre-K to Sixth Grade in New York State

GRADE	GEOMETRY CLUSTER	GEOMETRY CLUSTER
PK	Identify and describe shapes (squares, circles, triangles, rectangles).	Analyze, compare, and sort objects.
K	Identify and describe shapes.	Analyze, compare, create, and compose shapes.
1	Reason with shapes and their attributes.	None
2	Reason with shapes and their attributes.	None
3	Reason with shapes and their attributes.	None
4	Draw and identify lines and angles, and classify shapes by properties of their lines and angles.	None
5	Graph points on the coordinate plane to solve real-world and mathematical problems.	Classify two-dimensional figures into categories based on their properties.
6	Solve real-world and mathematical problems involving area, surface area, and volume.	None

Copyright © 2010 by National Governors Association Center for Best Practices and Council of Chief State School Officers. All rights reserved.

K–6 Standards for Mathematical Practice

There are eight SMPs, summarized in Hindu numerals 1 to 8:

1. Make sense of problems and persevere in solving them.
2. Reason abstractly and quantitatively.
3. Construct viable arguments and critique the reasoning of others.
4. Model with mathematics.
5. Use appropriate tools strategically.
6. Attend to precision.
7. Look for and make use of structure.
8. Look for and express regularity in repeated reasoning.

These eight SMPs are the same from kindergarten to 12th grade, but in New York State it begins earlier, in prekindergarten. The level of difficulty and complexity of each SMP is expected to increase as one goes up a grade. For example, with respect to SMP.2: Reason abstractly and quantitatively, a student assessed on 2.G.1 may identify and name a square shape and justify, *I know it is a square because it has four equal sides.* However, a student assessed on 5.G.3 would have much more to say about a square, such as, *a square is a 2-D shape and a parallelogram with four congruent angles and sides.*

The SMPs as written in the eight Roman numerals above are very concise summaries of the practice standards. Reading the shortened version without delving deeper into the meaning of each practice can lead to unnecessary misunderstandings. Thus, there is a need to comprehend and explore each SMP.

The early pages of the CCSSM book are a good resource to read to start unpacking the proposition of each SMP. These pages provide detailed explanations of how each SMP is to be understood. Other resources are websites such as:

- http://www.corestandards.org/Math/Practice/
- http://www.aea1.k12.ia.us/en/curriculum_instruction_and_assessment/math/iowa_core_resources/common_core_flip_books/

The second website provides a breakdown of each SMP by grade level and corresponding questions that can be posed to students that incorporate the SMP. Additionally, reading literature of how practitioners are thinking about SMPs or using SMPs is another valuable resource; for example, journal articles such as:

- Kastberg, S. E. (2014). Building mathematical practices: How many legs? *Teaching Children Mathematics, 20*(9), 538–540.
- Silbey, R. (2013). A closer look at mathematical practice 3: Explain and justify. *Teaching Children Mathematics, 20*(2), 70.
- Dacey, L., & Polly, D. (2012). CCSSM: The big picture. *Teaching Children Mathematics, 18*(6), 378–383.
- White, J., & Dauksas, L. (2012). CCSSM: Getting started K–grade 2. *Teaching Children Mathematics, 18*(7), 440–445.

In teaching and learning K–6 mathematics, both *content standards* and *practice standards* should be planned for and assessed. Awareness of the practice standards is important, and making it explicit in day-to-day lessons enables a deepening understanding of mathematics. Next, we describe four examples that incorporate both types of standards.

RP, OA, SMP.1, and SMP.6

Flo shops for birthday gifts all at once and has a budget of $100. As she selects items, Flo keeps a mental estimate of the total. The following are the items with prices in her cart: $25 iTunes Code; $27.99 Healthcare Grooming Kit; $39.19

Electric Toothbrush; $6.99 Ceramic Mug. Use estimation to decide if Flo will be over budget. Add the actual prices to check your estimate, calculate a 8% sales tax on the total, and present Flo with her actual bill.

An estimate of $99 is obtained by rounding to the nearest dollar. The estimate informs Flo that she is just under her budget, but the sales tax will push the total over her budget. Flo has a decision to make. Can she afford to be slightly over budget, or must she put an item back? The actual sum is required by the cashier to compute the appropriate sales tax and to charge Flo for her purchase.

This problem is an example of the purchases being almost equal to the budget. Students should be given a variety of these problems, and they should take the role of Flo and the cashier.

OA, SMP.4, and SMP.5

Boxes are piled up in the following manner:

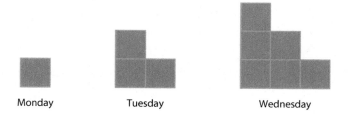

| Monday | Tuesday | Wednesday |

How many boxes will be in the pile on Thursday and Friday if the pattern continues? How many boxes are added each day? How long will it take to have enough boxes to fill a 10 × 10 warehouse?

Students can use manipulatives to help them figure out the pattern. Base-10 blocks would work well. The teacher could provide a blank chart for students to collect data; he or she could also ask students to make a conjecture about when the warehouse will be filled.

OA, SMP.7, and SMP.8

Three friends accidentally meet at a diner on October 1. Tom is at the diner every other day, Sue is at the diner every third day, and Brooke visits every fifth day. When will they meet at the diner again?

Different strategies can be used to solve this problem. Students can actually draw a calendar and mark when each person is at the diner. Another strategy is to mark each person's visit to the diner on a number line.

A solution should not signal the end of the problem for students. An ultimate objective is to have students provide questions that are prompted by the problem. In the example, an obvious question is when will the friends meet again for the third time?

Whichever strategy is used to find the first meeting, some students find that the LCM of the group of numbers is when the friends meet for the first time. After the first meeting, the friends find themselves together at the diner at multiples of the LCM.

OA, SMP.2, and SMP.3

When two numbers are added, is the sum even or odd?

First, students should collect some data (see Figure 3.2).

Figure 3.2: Data Generated by Students

$1 + 1 = 2$	$2 + 1 = 3$	$3 + 1 = 4$
$1 + 2 = 3$	$2 + 2 = 4$	$3 + 2 = 5$
$1 + 3 = 4$	$2 + 3 = 5$	$3 + 3 = 6$
$1 + 4 = 5$	$2 + 4 = 6$	$3 + 4 = 7$

The next step is for them to make general statements from their specific number sentences (inference). A student might make a statement that if both numbers being added are odd, then the sum is even. The student needs to justify her statement. She states that when using blocks to represent the numbers (Figure 3.3), a block can be taken from one set and placed with the other set. Each set now represents an even value (Figure 3.4). Whether the sets are taken separately or as a group, all the values are divisible by 2 or are even arrays.

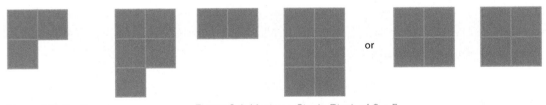

Figure 3.3: 3 + 5   Figure 3.4: Moving a Single Block of 3 + 5

Or the student could state that the block arrangements in Figure 3.3 could be joined together to form a 2×4 array (Figure 3.5). All even arrays represent even numbers.

Figure 3.5: A 2 × 4 Array

The opportunity for generalizing is now present; 2× (number) array is even because it can be separated into two equal groups. For the first explanation (Figure 3.2), a block is always missing in one array and an extra block is present in the other to make both arrays even arrays; therefore, exchanging a block makes both arrays even arrays. Both even arrays can be combined to make a larger even array (Figure 3.4). For the second explanation, the blocks in Figure 3.4 can always be rotated and joined like puzzle pieces to create the blocks in Figure 3.5. Therefore, adding two odd values results in an even value.

In conclusion to Section 3, a teacher candidate needs to recognize the curriculum's aims, goals, and understandings to be able to write a comprehensive and coherent lesson plan in order to effectively implement it. The mathematics curriculum standards covered in this section are the bare minimum concepts to be taught equitably to all students. These identified requirements are foundational ideas needed by elementary students for their future development of mathematics knowledge.

TERMS TO PONDER

Standard for mathematical practices	Content standard	Investigation
Domain	Central focus	Structures
Learning objective	Learning target	Model

ACTIVITY 3.1: What does each standard for mathematical practice (SMP) mean? How are teachers interpreting and using these SMPs?

ACTIVITY 3.2: Find and read this article: Bleiler, S. K., Baxter, W. A., Stephens, D. C., & Barlow, A. T. (2015). Constructing meaning: Standards for mathematical practice. *Teaching Children Mathematics, 21*(6), 336–334. Bleiler, et al. (2015) comment on the varied ways the SMP "model with mathematics" is deciphered. This raises the question of why we have common standards if different teachers can interpret the same SMP differently. What do you think?

ACTIVITY 3.3: In your own words, define *spiral, hierarchical, vertical,* and *horizontal curriculum.* Use Table 3.2

and the geometry standards (see CCSSM book or app) to provide specific example to support each definition.

www.explorelearning.com

Students/Teachers: Teachers can use this program with students in the classroom to work on math and science using interactive games and activities for grades 3 to 12. These Gizmos can be used on computers and tablets.

http://investigations-workshops.terc.edu

Teachers: This website offers workshops to teachers and leaders in the educational field. These workshops focus on professional development of areas in mathematics and science based on a specific curriculum. Through professional development, teachers, leaders, and administrators are able to implement specifically designed mathematics content and pedagogy in their schools.

www.mathcounts.org

Students: Math Counts is a website dedicated to the Math Counts Foundation, which supports math competitions, math clubs, and math video challenges for students at the middle school level. Through these three activities/programs, Math Counts empowers students of all ability levels to reach their full potential in mathematics.

www.arcademics.com

Students: Students can use this website for engaging in math practice through various arcade-like math games. Grades include first to sixth, and topics for games include shapes, counting, addition, subtraction, multiplication, division, integers, money, time, counting, decimals, fractions, ratios, algebra, and typing.

www.origoeducation.com

Teachers: ORIGO provides mathematical resources and professional learning to educators throughout the world. This website provides teachers with information on the ORIGO Program, which is a supplemental math program for grades 1 to 6. The website also provides information for professional development opportunities as well as games and visual aids that teachers can purchase for their classrooms.

https://www.illustrativemathematics.org

Teachers: Illustrative Math is a community of educators dedicated to coherent learning of mathematics. Teachers use this website to learn how to become a teacher of math in order to help students' comprehension. Using a variety of teacher resources shared among the community, teachers develop professionally in strategies and the Common Core Standards.

Assessment of Mathematics

Introduction

Assessment is gathering evidence based on an objective(s). Normally, a test is used to collect the evidence, and the collected information is then evaluated against some criteria for decision-making. Assessment is what moves student learning along; thus, it "is a valuable tool for making instructional decisions" (Principles and Standards, 2000, p. 22).

Features of Assessment

There are a number of reasons for assessing (see Table 4.1). Mainly the purpose of assessment in a classroom is to monitor student progress to inform the student and teacher about growth toward a mathematical learning target. At times teachers assess to make instructional decisions, such as whether to move on to complex math concepts or reengage the students using different strategies, or simply to evaluate student achievement.

Assessment is a four-step process that involves (a) planning out clear objectives, (b) collecting evidence via one of the multiple tools and methods, (c) interpreting evidence or making inferences, and (d) applying the results to make decisions.

Table 4.1: Summary of Assessment Aspects

PURPOSE OF ASSESSMENT	To gauge students' readiness to learn To gauge students' comprehension of concepts, facts, skills, and procedures To gauge whether students need to practice, be retaught, or be reengaged To gauge student reasoning or problem-solving ability
TYPE OF ASSESSMENT	Formative, summative, informal, formal, pretest and posttest, pre-assessment, post-assessment, diagnostic predictive, aptitude, standardized test—criterion referenced, norm referenced
ASSESSMENT TOOL OR INSTRUMENTS	1-minute paper, digital tools such as apps and software, observation checklist, oral presentation, self-rating rubric, exit ticket, written reflection, test, quiz, analytic rubric, thumbs-up or thumbs-down, holistic rubric, interview, worksheet, conference
STUDENT ASSESSED	Individually or independently, small group, partner, whole class
ASSESSMENT APPROACH	Process or product based, continuous or final in nature, divergent or convergent in thinking

Categories of Assessments

As seen in Table 4.1, there are numerous types of assessments. In mathematics what should be assessed are concepts, facts, skills, procedures, problem-solving processes, justification, and reasoning skills. Mostly, formative and summative assessments are employed in teaching and learning of mathematics. Brief discussions of these categories of assessment are considered in this section.

A *summative assessment* is information gathered once the goal, learning segment, unit, and so on is complete; for example, chapter tests, examinations, unit tests, formal diagnostic math, one-on-one interviews.

A *formative assessment* is information gathered before, during, or at the end of a lesson. Formative assessments work throughout the entire lesson, since they are quick checks. A teacher can have students draw or use an exit ticket, or assign homework, quiz, think-pair-share, thumbs-up or thumbs-down, personal whiteboards, 1-minute paper, and so on. For example, a 1-minute paper can be used in the introduction to summarize a previously assigned reading. The 1-minute paper can be used in the main body of the lesson to explain or justify students' thinking. A formative assessment at the lesson's closure allows students to list one thing they don't understand via a 1-minute paper.

The 1-minute paper is an assessment tool; the question or problem given to the student is the assessment and is aligned to an objective. There must be a reason or purpose for posing the question, the *criterion* (*criteria*, plural). The decision you make as a teacher of the student's response to the posed question is the *evaluation*. So based on some measures, you can make the judgment call whether the student has met the objective or not. Beware of what to look for (criterion) when assessing, be it verbally, in written form, or merely observing as you circulate in the class during group work or seat work.

Evaluation

To be able to measure what we are looking for, a rubric is designed. A rubric is an evaluation criteria or scale used for scoring student performance on a test or task. A teacher can use either a holistic scoring rubric or analytic scoring rubric; using rubrics requires the ability to spell out the criterion or criteria to be evaluated that is aligned to assessment objectives.

The ability to write down, in complete sentences, certain and specific math notions embedded in learning tasks—such as questions, word problems, and activities—is useful in writing reports, student feedback, or notes for parent–teacher conferences.

Examples of CRITERIA across Common Core's ten math domains

CC—Counting and Cardinality

- Arranges numbers up to 10 in order of magnitude
- List combinations of 5
- Matches picture quantities with the correct number
- Names and writes numerals

NBT—Number and Operations in Base Ten

- Estimates product by rounding factors
- Multiplies a number by powers of 10
- Compares the least of two quantities, up to 1,000
- Rounds to the nearest hundredths

OA—Operations and Algebraic Thinking

- Recognizes compatible sums of 50
- Solves story problem on addition

- Describes strategy using pictures and words for solving an equation
- Divides a four-digit number by a two-digit number with a remainder

G—Geometry

- Composes and decomposes shapes
- Describes bilateral and rotational symmetry
- Classifies polygons using number of sides
- Calculates surface area of tetrahedron

RP—Ratios and Proportional Relationships

- Distinguishes between ratios and rates
- Solves real-world problems using proportionality
- Computes discount amount
- Fills missing values in a time–distance table

MD—Measurement and Data

- Measures length using nonstandard unit without gaps, overlap and end-to-end
- Accurately coverts grams to kilograms and vice versa
- Uses the formula $V = b \times h$ to evaluate volume of a square prism
- Draws a bar graph of data on classmates' favorite fruit

NF—Number and Operations: Fractions

- Changes improper fraction to mixed fraction
- Justifies the relative size of fractions with the same numerator but with different denominators
- Represents equivalent fractions on a number line
- Uses visual fraction model to multiply a fraction by a whole number

EE—Expressions and Equations

- Simplifies numerical expressions using PEMDAS
- Provides real-world examples of independent and dependent variables
- Correctly writes an inequality based on a given word problem
- Evaluates an expression by substituting given values

SP—Statistics and Probability

- Draws a histogram
- Computes measures of averages of a given set of data
- Writes conclusion of what a graph depicts
- Describes distribution of data—shape, gap, peaks, clusters, outliers

NS—The Number System

- Accurately computes quotients involving divisors to the hundredths
- Uses integers to plot coordinate points in any quadrant
- Finds LCM (least common multiple) of three numbers up to 50
- Solves real-world problems with division of a fraction by another fraction

Assessment and Data-Driven Instruction

Data-driven instruction is critical in the 21st century in all areas of education, from daily classroom instruction to programmatic or institutional assessment. In a classroom learning context, a teacher should list the objectives of the assessment; write the assessment; write the evaluation criteria; administer the assessment; analyze the assessment; and reflect, evaluate, and act on the teaching and learning implications noted. We give an illustration of *assessment objectives* that are aligned to the *assessment*, the *evaluation criteria* in Table 4.2, the *quantitative analysis of assessment* in Table 4.3, and a *bar graph of a classroom assessment* in Figure 4.1:

Assessment Objectives

1. Student will be able to estimate the product of a two-digit whole number with a decimal to the hundredths using rounding to the nearest ones.
2. Student will be able to calculate the product of a two-digit whole number with a decimal to the hundredths using an appropriate efficient procedure.
3. Student will be able to compare the reasonableness of estimated product to the actual product using place value

Assessment

1) A slice of pizza costs $1.57. How much does 27 slices cost?
2) (i) Round factors to estimate the product of 6.47×63
   (ii) Multiply 6.47×63 by showing your work.
   (iii) Compare your two answers in part (i) and (ii). Explain.

Numbers 1 and 2 of this assessment cover a total of four questions that deal with a concept, a procedure, and both problem-solving and reasoning skills as stated in the objectives above. In short, the assessment looks at all the mathematical understandings; namely, conceptual understanding, procedural fluency, mathematical reasoning, and problem solving.

Evaluation Criteria

Table 4.2: Evaluation Criteria

CRITERIA	EXCEEDS TARGET	MEETS TARGET	LIMITED PROGRESS
Estimate product by rounding factors	Rounds factors to the nearest ones to find closest estimate to the actual product	Rounds factors to compatible numbers to estimate the product	No estimate OR Underestimates OR Overestimates
Uses long division, tape diagram, ... to find actual product of 2-digit numbers with a decimal	Uses appropriate procedure and gets the actual product	Uses appropriate procedure and has correct partial products but places the decimal point incorrectly	Uses appropriate procedure but misaligns place value AND/OR has incorrect product
Uses appropriate units and decimal place	Correctly labels cost with $ and leaves it to the nearest hundredths	Correctly labels cost with $ and does not leave it to the nearest hundredths	Does not OR incorrectly labels cost AND/OR rounds it up or down
Justifies the closeness of the estimate to actual product	Explains the difference between the estimate and actual is small because of rounding to the nearest ones	Explains the difference between the estimate and actual is close because of rounding to the nearest tens	Does not explain the difference between the estimate and actual OR Underestimates OR Overestimates

Quantitative Analysis of Classroom Assessment

Table 4.3: Aggregated Quantitative Analysis of Classroom Assessment

CRITERIA	EXCEEDS TARGET	MEETS TARGET	LIMITED PROGRESS
Estimate product by rounding factors	40% (n = 21)	55% (n = 21)	5% (n = 21)
Uses long division, tape diagram, ... to find actual product of 2-digit numbers with a decimal	85% (n = 21)	10% (n = 21)	5% (n = 21)
Uses appropriate units and decimal place	30% (n = 21)	60% (n = 21)	10% (n = 21)
Justifies the closeness of the estimate to actual product	10% (n = 21)	80% (n = 21)	10% (n = 21)

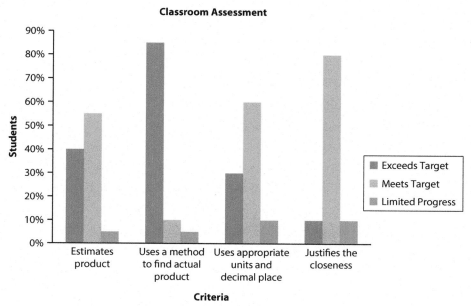

Classroom Assessment

Figure 4.1: Bar Graph of Student Performance on Formative Assessment

Assessment of Learning Segment on Decimals

An example of an assessment of a three-lesson learning segment for Grade 5, EngageNY Module 2 on Topic C: Decimal Multi-Digit Multiplication of the NYS Common Core is discussed. The lesson segment addresses the Common Core Standard 5.NBT.7:

> Add, subtract, multiply, and divide decimals to hundredths, using concrete models or drawings and strategies based on place value, properties of operations, and/or the relationship between addition and subtraction; relate the strategy to a written method and explain the reasoning used. (5th Grade Mathematics Module 2, NYS CSSS, EngageNY.org, 2.c.1)

The Lesson's Objective

- Lesson 1: Multiply decimal fractions with hundredths by a multi-digit whole number using place value understanding to record partial products.
- Lesson 2: Multiply decimal fractions with hundredths by a multi-digit whole number through conversion to a whole number problem and reasoning about the placement of the decimal.

- Lesson 3: Justification of the product of a whole number and a decimal with hundredths using place value understanding and estimation.

Six multi-digit multiplication problems and four application problems were selected (see the appendix "Decimal Tests"). The appendix contains a class set of simulated assessments. Directions asked students to estimate the product of the multi-digit multiplication problems. The concept being tested throughout the assessment was accurate placement of the decimal point. Obtaining the correct product of a multi-digit multiplication problem without decimal location addressed procedural fluency. Asking students to estimate products aided in determining the reasonableness of the answer while assessing this valuable skill. Word problems allowed students to show their problem-solving skills.

Once the test is administered, it needs scoring, and feedback should be provided.

Figure 4.2 shows an example of written feedback to sample student work.

As the quizzes are reviewed, errors and misunderstandings should be noted. In organizing the data, a chart should be constructed with criteria that reflect alignment with the assessment's objectives. The criteria for evaluation can vary; that is, accuracy in multiplying and correct decimal placement in every problem may be a good indicator of mastery if those were the foci.

6.47 × 63 6.47 63 1941 3882 40761.00	**Written feedback:** You have correctly used the long multiplication, Student A, but you may want to move the decimal point two places to the right. I would like you to estimate your product first before carrying the multiplication. The estimation helps you to make comparison with the actual answer i.e. Rounding the factors to 6 and 60 shows you that the actual product will be above 360 and 6 and 70 shows it will be below 420.
Written feedback: Student A, you used the long multiplication correctly but you placed your decimal point in the incorrectly, by moving it two places to the right instead of the left. I would like to meet with you to review multiplication and division by powers of ten.	$ 1.57. How much does 27 slices cost? $1.57 27 1099 314 $4239.00

Figure 4.2: Written Feedback

Table 4.4: Disaggregate Data of Student Performance

	PLACEMENT OF THE DECIMAL POINT	ACCEPTABLE INTERPRETATION OF PROBLEM	APPROPRIATE MULTIPLICATION PROCEDURE	REASONABLE ESTIMATES AND PRODUCT
Student 1				
Student 2				
...				

Correct estimation includes a variety of acceptable answers for the first six problems. Multiplying unrounded numbers or incorrect rounding denotes difficulty in estimating and should be counted as incorrect.

After reviewing the assessments and constructing the chart, a summary (aggregated data) can be made of conceptual understanding of the place value concept, procedural fluency in multiplication using an acceptable algorithm, problem solving of the word problems, and reasoning skills.

Table 4.5: Aggregated Data of Assessment

CRITERIA	EXCEPTIONAL	PROFICIENT	NOVICE
Placement of the decimal point			
Acceptable interpretation of problem			
Reasonable estimates and product			
Appropriate multiplication procedure			

The qualitative description should include the areas in which the entire class excelled and struggled. The discussion can be couched in the general prior knowledge the class possesses; for example, multiplication accuracy and completion of the quiz were hampered by the general struggle to master multiplication facts.

The analysis should specifically address errors, confusions, and partial understandings in as much detail as possible. In evaluating the assessment, you may note students with specific learning need not providing more details in their work, the gifted students who don't see the need to show their work or to estimate, students who are struggling with these concepts, and so forth. If the students have the same misunderstandings, structuring a follow-up lesson on a math area of struggle is easier.

For example, although students F, G, J, P, and R show fluency in multiplying multi-digit numbers, they are locating the decimal by counting from the left. State an objective for correcting the misunderstandings of these students. Remember, the assessment for the follow-up lesson will be aligned to this objective (multiplying and dividing a number by powers of 10). In situations where the area of struggle is the content already taught in class, the follow-up lesson plan will require employment of new strategies and learning tasks. Repeating the same lesson or going over the quiz are not educationally effective strategies for helping these struggling students. The lesson plan should specifically address what the students will be doing and what the instructor will be doing, and a change of representation could be a help to the students; for example:

$$10(0.1) = 0.1 + 0.1 + 0.1 + 0.1 + 0.1 + 0.1 + 0.1 + 0.1 + 0.1 + 0.1 = 1.0$$

Therefore, $10(0.1) = 1.0$; a conceptual representation that shows a justification for the location of the decimal point. Use formative assessments to measure performance and analyze the effectiveness of strategies employed in reengagement lessons, as well as to evaluate the impact on the bigger mathematical picture of the targeted standards.

In concluding this section on assessment, we would like to point out to teacher candidates that assessment is significant in teaching since it enables practitioners to reflect upon their practice, whether it is reflection in practice or reflection on practice.

Responding positively to the results and to the implications of analyzed assessments is what counts as being an effective teacher—it is the core of data-driven instruction.

TERMS TO PONDER		
Criterion	Formative	Pre-assessment
Aggregated data	Summative	Feedback
Grading	Scores	Answer sheet
Analytic rubric	Portfolio	Worksheet
Activity	Reengagement	Pretest

ACTIVITY 4.1: Distinguish between holistic versus analytic rubric.

ACTIVITY 4.2: Compare and contrast test, assessment, and evaluation using a three-set Venn diagram.

ACTIVITY 4.3: There are archived annotated exams on EngageNY and NYSED.gov (testing) that you can use to garner expertise in unpacking CCSS standards relative to an assessment question and build a repertoire of description of math concepts, facts, procedures, and skills. Look at the sample questions, answers, and commentaries on the EngageNY website (http://www.engageny.org/resource/new-york-state-common-core-sample-questions). This activity empowers you to be able to identify and name the students' areas of math strengths or misconceptions or partial mathematics understanding in a student work sample.

ACTIVITY 4.4: Work with any K–6 math standard(s) to design an assessment to evaluate student learning. Write a comprehensive assessment aligned with objectives. Then, practice writing, adopting, or adapting an assessment that covers the four dimensions of mathematical understandings (*conceptual understanding, procedural fluency, mathematical reasoning,* and *problem solving*), with the focus on quality not quantity.

◊ If you would like to *write* or *adapt* an assessment, use Bleiler and Thompson's (2012) SPUR framework on multidimensional assessment—**SPUR** stands for **S**kills, **P**roperties, **U**ses, and **R**epresentation.

◊ Use Bleiler and Thompson's (2012) question, "Was the assessment balanced across the four dimensions?" (p. 299) if *adopting* an assessment.

ACTIVITY 4.5: Practice writing up a rubric, an evaluation criteria, to grade the assessment in Activity 4.4. Write an *analytic* rubric that is aligned to the objectives of your assessment. Note that the evaluation criteria can be in any format, but the analytic rubric gives an opportunity to explore varied patterns of learning and enables you to easily provide both quantitative and qualitative description and analysis of the student's performance on the whole-class assessment.

ACTIVITY 4.6: Practice grading, giving feedback, and analyzing student work. Providing verbal or written feedback based on the evaluation criteria is important for students to know with respect to the learning target.

◊ Practice writing useful feedback on the students' work by applying the criteria identified in the rubric and also for consistency with all of the students' work. Writing "good" or "awesome" is not useful feedback to a student if not qualified by a constructive statement. Writing, "Good, I see you have written the word problem using an equation with the letter x standing for the unknown vehicles" is useful feedback. You need to identify what the student has done well and what the student needs to work on toward solving the problem. Give hints to improve work and for the next steps forward.

ACTIVITY 4.7: Analyze students' work to find strengths and deficits in the work. You are encouraged to use Lamberg's (2013) questions when analyzing:

◊ What do you think [*Student A*] understands?

◊ What errors or misconceptions do [*Student A*] have?

◊ What could be a potential focus topic for … [reengaging *Student A*]? (p. 84)

You must look to see how the students have performed on *conceptual understanding, procedural fluency, mathematical reasoning,* and *problem solving.* "Do the results suggest that a greater focus of … instruction should be devoted to a particular dimension of understanding?" (Bleiler & Thompson, 2012, p. 299).

Websites

www.mathisfun.com   *Grade 1–7*: Algebra, data, geometry, measure, number, dictionary, games, puzzles, and worksheets.

www.funbrain.com: *Grade K–6*: Math arcade, math baseball, tic-tac-toe squares, vine time, Sudoku, connect the dots.

www.studyladder.com   *Grade K–6*: Number and place value, mental math, fractions and decimals, patterns and algebra, data, chance and probability, time, length, area, volume, mass, angles, 3-D, transformations, dictionary.

www.mathplayground.com   *Grade K–6*: Games, arcade, logic, videos, word problems, learning activities, Sticky Linky, Jelly Slice, Cat Around Africa, Monsterland, Hexagonator, problem solving, manipulatives.

www.hoodamath.com   *Students*: This website provides mathematics games and activities for students to use to practice developing their math skills. Games and activities cover a variety of math topics that can be used for a variety of ages from kindergarten to high school.

www.learningupgrade.com (songs, videos, games)—*Students:* Students can learn math through the Common Core math standards using games, videos, and songs that are aligned with the standards. Games, songs, and videos can be used in whole-group or individualized instruction.

www.mymathbuddies.com *Tools:* Marshal Cavendish Education is the organization that established Math Buddies, a digital complement to today's math textbooks. With its interrelated components, Math Buddies supports the development of five intertwined strands that help students develop proficiency in math: conceptual understanding, procedural competence, strategic competence, adaptive reasoning, and productive disposition.

Managing the Mathematics Classroom

Introduction

This section provides a brief discussion of the mathematics classroom. Fruitful teaching and learning of mathematics requires a safe learning environment that permits mutual interactions, respectful communication, and good rapport among all. Thus, creation of sociomathematical norms for interaction is key. A teacher must be a good classroom manager for this to happen. There are numerous things to manage, including students, content, assessment, time, physical classroom arrangement, materials, and resources. In this section, we will predominantly focus on classroom environment.

Classroom Learning Environment

Managing the learning environment is as important as conveying conceptual understanding. A chaotic, disruptive class often makes learning extremely difficult for most students. Classroom management is best thought of from a problem-solving viewpoint. What can I do to ensure the learning environment is safe for all?

Procedures are essential. Procedures need to be in place for leaving the room as a group, leaving the room as an individual, going to the bathroom, going to lunch, getting ready to go outside, returning to the classroom from outside, obtaining supplies for a task, cleaning up, working in a group, working alone, when students can talk, when students need to be quiet, arriving for the day, and leaving at the end of the day. Procedures need to be explained, including expectations of the students' behavior, and they need to be practiced. Depending on the grade level, procedures need to be re-explained frequently throughout the school year.

First, you are the authority. You need not be mean, but you do have to demand that students abide by the rules. Set high expectations for learning as well as behavior. Convey that there is no time for fooling around; the important reason students are in your class is to improve as democratic citizens. Show confidence: You know your expectations, you learned in an excellent elementary education program, and you prepare well for each day.

Part of the learning environment is physical. Thought needs to be given to the arrangement of the room and furniture. Where are the high-traffic areas? Will there be a resource area or a quiet area? Is there space for students to share? Is there space for learning stations, a learning center, or a bulletin board? Is there a space or section for posters that are changed on a weekly basis or with each unit? Too many posters on the wall can be distracting, so look for a balance.

Part of the learning environment is mental. What can you do to ensure that your students feel safe? Mistakes are a natural part of learning. Do students have a growth mindset and take mistakes in stride? Are students encouraged to persevere in tasks they work on? Do students take mental risks? Essentially, effort is what you want to value. Effort shows that students believe they can accomplish the task at hand. Effort allows talented students to go a bit further. Effort lends to the thinking that all is possible. Everyone can read, write, and create mathematics.

Be on the lookout for students who say they can't do a task because they have not been taught how. A student with a growth mindset will attempt any task. As the daily climate takes place, it accumulates into a culture, so what happens daily is what generally is expected to happen. Established cultures are difficult to change; make yours positive. Proactively find ways to motivate appropriate behavior, such as by establishing the *Bucket Filler* norm—which is a positive reinforcement plan where a student is nominated for performing an act of kindness or good actions that fill another person's bucket. Such a plan can be effectively implemented in cooperative and collaborative learning tasks.

There will be days when every part of the day does not go as planned. You need to be flexible and adjust. Again, classroom management is about problem solving. Why didn't the plan work? Is there an alternate way to approach what needs to be accomplished? Is the plan of action really worth it?

The best of all possible situations is that students internalize a code of conduct incorporating "do what is right." With the goal of students taking responsibility for their actions, your job is to give plenty of positive feedback when correct behavior is observed. Most students are somewhere on the continuum of trying to follow the rules to always doing what is right.

Classroom rules, established via group discussion, give the best structure to classroom management. Rules should be written in a positive manner, be few in number, and be posted. Consequences are needed if rules are broken. A gradual increase in severity makes giving a consequence bearable and helps stop small problems before they escalate. A look or other nonverbal cue, proximity, a brief reminder of appropriate behavior, a one-to-one conference, a time out, and a call home are examples of a consequence stream. You know that if a student is having a rough day, he or she may get to the end of the stream. Consider how many steps to include in the rules—(a) a warning system; (b) action to take, say, isolation; (c) a consequence, such as no recess; and (d) if behavior continues, maybe a visit to the principal's office before calling home.

Together with the student, make a plan for improved behavior. Students need to acknowledge that they are the disruption, and then they can make suggestions on how they can improve their behavior. Teachers, in general, have to get over being uncomfortable about confronting a misbehaving student. The mantra is to be assertive. Your job is to keep the learning environment suitable for deep cognitive engagement. There is no sense in having rules if you are unwilling to follow through when they are broken.

Developing relations, rapport, and respect with students is an important part of a teacher's daily routine. Relationships can remain intact even when dealing with a classroom management issue. Address the issue and then move on. A clean slate is again established; character has been built.

Interactions between students need to be carefully monitored. Bullying can't be tolerated; therefore, it is necessary to observe interactions to be aware if any are hurtful. Immediate action needs to take place if bullying is discovered.

Misbehavior generally is not about you, the teacher; it is not personal. Remember, the student has chosen to act in an inappropriate manner or present a poor attitude. Students have many social interactions that take place outside the classroom. The effects of unhealthy relationships manifest themselves in class. Sometimes students misbehave because they didn't get what they wanted or didn't get to do what they wanted; but other times, students just want to get out of doing something.

Teachers always need to be mindful that they can be a disrupter, too. Yelling at a classroom full of students is an indicator that insufficient monitoring has been done. Many times teachers try to talk over student noise. Waiting for quiet allows your message to be heard and your voice to last until the end of the day. In resolving issues, deescalate emotions and manage anger using simple techniques like taking three deep breaths or silently humming the happy birthday song.

Remember, take care of the small problems so large problems don't develop. Cultivate a sense of *with-it-ness*. By observation, you need to know what is going on in all areas of your classroom. Don't be distracted.

Even when helping a student or group of students, you need to be aware of what your other students are doing. As the commercial stated, "You have 200 degrees of sight. Good for you. Bad for the Barkley twins." Constantly beware of what is happening in the classroom. It is important to know, monitor, prevent, and nip the misbehavior in the bud, rather than waiting, which can end in disaster.

Managing Mathematics Instruction

A safe class environment will enhance teaching and learning of mathematics, but its presence alone does not imply automatic effective instruction. A teacher must also manage math instruction. Here are a few tips:

- To settle students down for a lesson, try "bellringer," "eye opener," "hook," or "do now."
- Plan ways to call on students at random. Each student should be alert and attentive at all times if such a plan exists, and not just a few perpetual vocal participants. An example of this technique would be, the "popsicle method"—calling student names written on a popsicle stick—or "cold calling."
- Plan ways to gain insight to student's reasoning, such as a "show me."
- Plan for active participation by using thumbs-up or thumbs-down, choral unison response, think-pair-share, erasable markers and 8 × 11 whiteboards, and so on.
- For small group management, give clear directions: take turns; use quiet voices; stay with the group; what to do when done; specify division of work; assign roles—reporter, elaborator, gatherer, checker, any needed role.
- For whole-class attention, try the following: eyes on me; pens down; calling out loud the class's pet name or nickname and requiring a unison response from students (for example, "Mathematicians!" "Class-class!"); clapping hands; snapping fingers; count backward from 3 to 1.
- Plan ways to transition from one task to the other, such as counting backward from 10 to 1.
- For reinforcement—for an oral presentation, try whole class silent cheering, waving or shaking both hands, or snapping fingers.
- When starting an activity, be sure to give the direction first. A good strategy is to have a student explain what she or he has heard as the directions. Then, have students get into groups and distribute materials. Try to be quiet except for the formative assessment questions you will be asking students as they complete the activity, such as "Can you explain what you are doing?" and "Why are you doing that?"

- Time management is imperative; otherwise, closure of a lesson never gets properly implement as planned.
- And much more: We say "much more" because it is true. More management paraphernalia, say, administratively: Remember to make enough copies of the activity for the whole class, take attendance, collect students' work, score and provide written feedback, record grades, analyze grades, and return students' work.

In conclusion to this section on the mathematics classroom, we would like to point out that being an effective teacher calls for inculcating a robust leadership and developing assertive managerial skills. Teaching and learning thrives in safe classroom environments; thus, structure must be in place for it to happen.

TERMS TO PONDER		
Sociomathematical norms	With-it-ness	1-minute paper
Bellringer	Hook	Eye-opener
Teaching philosophy	Rapport	Respect
Mutual respect	Learning center	Cold calling

ACTIVITY 5.1: Write your classroom management philosophy.

ACTIVITY 5.2: Begin to imagine the sociomathematical norm to cultivate. Journal it.

ACTIVITY 5.3: Discuss the strategies you will use to (a) get every student's attention, (b) keep students on task, and (c) manage the needs of multiple students.

ACTIVITY 5.4: Will you have a poster for independent work when a student is finished with assigned task? If yes, write it. How about directions to small group work? If yes, write it.

ACTIVITY 5.5: Sketch your physical class arrangement aligned to your teaching philosophy.

www.mathlanding.org

Teachers: This website provides resources and tools for elementary math specialists and teachers. When registered on the site, members can create and join groups, participate in discussion forums, upload resources to share with others, rate and comment on resources, and find and organize resources into personal folders. Teachers are able to collaborate with other professionals and find math tools and resources to bring into their own classroom.

www.reflexmath.com

Students/Teachers: Reflex is a program that teachers can use with their students in order to assess students' knowledge of math facts. Students grade 2 and above can use Reflex to test their knowledge in various areas of math, such as addition, subtraction, multiplication, and division. Teachers are able to track student progress and well as monitor their improvement.

www.mathincontext.eb.com

Teachers: This website has information on Mathematics in Context (MiC), a comprehensive mathematics curriculum for middle school students. Instruction and content of the curriculum follow the Common Core State Standards, individual state standards, and the Principles and Standards for School Mathematics according to the National Council of Teachers of Mathematics. Units covered include ratios, proportions, geometry, algebra, probability, and statistics.

www.cpm.org

CPM Is an educational nonprofit organization dedicated to improving grades 6–12 mathematics instruction. CPM offers professional development and curriculum materials that follow the Common Core State Standards. The site provides helpful information for teachers, students, and parents, with links for professional development, resources, homework help, related studies, parent guides, and much more.

www.borenson.com

Tools: This website provides a supplemental way for teachers to teach students how to solve various math problems using a pictorial and visual approach. The hands-on methods are for grades 3 to 8 and help students with solving algebra equations. Workshops, videos, and research information pertaining to this whole-brain instructional approach are available on the website

www.conceptuamath.com

Teachers: Conceptua Math is a curriculum that teachers can purchase and use in their classrooms with students in grades K to 8 of varying ability levels. This curriculum is an online visually interactive math curriculum. The website provides insight into the curriculum, providing lesson framework, Common Core alignment, adaptability for teachers, case studies, research information, and much more.

Resources for Teaching Mathematics

Introduction

There are many tools and resources that can be used in mathematics, such as children's literature, manipulatives, textbooks, lesson plan templates, math dictionaries, maps, posters, bulletin boards, desktop computers, handheld computers, calculators, interactive whiteboards, classroom response systems, digital cameras, video cameras, CDs, apps, cell phones, online resources, blogs, MP3s, DVDs, wikis, social media, and so on. In this section, we will look at some of these technologies briefly— literature, manipulatives, digital media, calculators, software, websites, and lesson plan templates.

Children's Literature Books

Children's literature books help communicate mathematics in story form. Stories bring meaning and help make connection to real-world life, eradicating any abstractness in most cases. Again, stories are fun and capture both students' interest and curiosity. Aside from motivating and making authentic connections to mathematics, a teacher can use children literature in countless ways. Some examples follow:

- To introduce a concept; for instance, *Math Count: Capacity* by Henry Pluckrose, a Children's Press publication

- In a problem-solving task; for instance, *Ready, Set, Hop!* by Stuart J. Murphy, a HarperCollins publication
- To document the history of mathematics; for instance, *Calculators* by Jan P. Haney, a Raintree publication
- To bring in a cultural aspect of mathematics; for instance, the *Count Your Way* series
- To model mathematics; for instance, "Smart," a poem by Shel Silverstein, http://learn.fi.edu/pieces/knox/smart.htm
- Interdisciplinary purposes; for instance, *The Grouchy Ladybug* by Eric Carle, a HarperCollins publication
- Create an extension activity; for instance, *Earth Day—Hooray* by Stuart J. Murphy, a HarperCollins publication

The majority of children literature books are read aloud in YouTube videos, making it readily available for whole-class viewing and discussion. Teachers can pause the video at any point to pose questions or actively engage the students in a task before moving further into the reading.

Manipulatives

Manipulatives provide hands-on learning and also enable modeling of mathematics. They are great for problem-based learning and experiential learning. Examples of manipulatives are base-10 blocks, attribute blocks, pattern blocks, tangrams, supertangrams, pentaminoes, spinners, rulers, mira, capacity containers, decimal squares, cubes, fake money, balance scale, color tiles, Cuisenaire rods, 10-frames, dice, playing cards, protractor, fraction squares, fraction bars, fraction circles, clock face, and dominoes. Some of these manipulatives can be found in both concrete and virtual forms (e-manipulatives). In the National Library of Virtual Manipulatives, one of the manipulatives is a geoboard. Students can investigate perimeter and area of any figure they create. Another problem that can be posed for the geoboard is how many line segments of different lengths can be formed.

There are many factory-manufactured manipulatives, but a teacher can create them or improvise using *realia* or recyclables such as egg cartons to teach fractions or things that come in groups for multiplication or soup cans for teaching how to find surface areas of closed cylinders, open cylinders, and pipes.

Note that a manipulative can be used teach different math concepts. This is a key reason why a teacher needs to be explicit and clear in stating directions to a learning task involving use of a manipulative. For example, using pattern blocks gives a good illustration of this, since they can be used to teach sorting and classification, angles, tessellations, patterns, shapes, perimeter, congruency, and fractions—wholes, $\frac{1}{2}, \frac{1}{3}, \frac{1}{6}$, or any combinations of these benchmark fractions. Thus, if you want students to work on adding fractions using pattern blocks, say so and proceed to demonstrate how to do so; otherwise, some students may focus on the shapes or the beauty of the colors.

The dual natures of manipulatives call for a teacher to scaffold an activity that uses these materials. In facilitation, put emphasis on the relationship between the concrete illustration and the math symbolization. The direction to the learning task, if based on investigation, must be clear to help bridge the tangible hands-on object to the intangible and abstract math idea or concept.

Lesson Plan Templates

There are many templates for planning a lesson, and this is dictated by the prevailing teaching philosophy. A template for an inquiry-based lesson is different from a direct-instruction template. However, any given lesson plan must have three things; namely, the introduction, the main body, and the closure. These core parts, *intro-body-closure*, of a lesson are named in different ways in different lesson plan templates; for example, *bring-do-leave, launch-explore-summarize, before-during-after*, and so on.

Again, different templates divide each of the core lesson plan parts into more subsections. The approach used in a lesson dictates the necessary and the unnecessary subsections. The requirements of an exploratory lesson are different from an expository lesson.

Aside from having the core parts of a lesson, there are some important considerations that a teacher must look into. Pay attention to the following:

- Equity and culturally responsive teaching
- Developmental age appropriateness:—concept, language, social, physical, emotional
- Management of content—be it strategies, procedures, or transitions
- Seating arrangement—accommodations versus classroom interaction
- Management of time—plan time and make students aware during the instruction how much time they have for each task. It is crucial to bring the lesson to closure, so beware when time is running out.
- Instructional approaches—discovery learning, lecture, discussion, exploration, peer tutoring, hands-on activities, cooperative learning, questioning, technology-based approach, interdisciplinary instruction, problem-based learning

A lesson plan should be prepared for one day. If the concept or idea requires more time to complete, then a series of lesson plans are sequenced consecutively. A series of lessons with the same idea is called a *learning segment* or a *unit plan,* and the theme thereof is the *central focus.*

Description of sample subsections (italicized) of a lesson plan template

Remember that for a particular lesson plan, your language should be explicit, exact, and specific, not general or broad. We will describe possible subsections of a lesson plan in each paragraph:

Demographics and learning context: Teacher candidate name, date, grade level, lesson plan title, time required for lesson, number of boys and girls, students' needs assessment, student interests, community assets and culture, and so on.

Common Core State Standard(s)/NYS Standards: Copy its code number and text description. Include both *content* standard as well as standards for mathematical *practice* (SMP).

Learning objectives versus learning target: Ensure the learning objectives and learning targets are aligned to the chosen standards and the assessments and are student centered. Use the *ABCD strategy* for writing objectives:

- *A* = Audience: The student not teacher; use the sentence frame "The student will be able to ..." (SWBAT).
- *B* = Behavior: What a student is expected to be able to do. The behavior should be measurable or observable; for example, write, represent, explain, estimate, solve, construct, build, compare, tally.
- *C* = Condition: The given condition or situation under which the work is to occur.
- *D* = Degree: The acceptable level of performance.

Examples of learning objectives include: (a) The student will be able to identify numerical patterns correctly using four given rules; and (b) By the end of this lesson, the student will be able to draw objects and write their numeral after viewing the images of *Anno's Counting Book* by Mitsumasa Anno.

What then, are *learning targets?* They are objectives written from a student perspective or student voice utilizing *I can* statements without the SWBAT; for example, (a) I can use the *AB AB* rule to list three missing values in a pattern arrangement; and (b) I can draw a picture to show any number of objects from 1 to 10 like in the *Counting Book* story.

Multiple assessment strategies: Ensure you assess concepts, facts, procedures, and problem-solving or reasoning skills verbally, in written form, or both. Observe, use think-pair-share, 1-minute paper, KWL, quiz, completing graphic organizer, and so on. Align the objectives of the assessment to the learning objectives.

The assessment could be any combination of the following: pre-assessment, formative, formal, informal, or summative assessment. Provide students the option to self-assess with respect to the learning target.

Materials needed: Tools and resources needed to teach the lesson and for *students to use as support* as needed; for example, artifacts, DVD, calculator, software, textbook, computer, exit slip, and anchor chart. Have enough worksheets, handouts, directions to the activity, and so on for the entire class.

Technology integration: Electronic whiteboard, e-manipulative, online resources, digital media, or calculators. State how the technology chosen is to be used in the lesson. Listing the technology does not communicate intention of usage; for example, there are many ways a Smart Board can be used in a lesson; thus, always specify how it is to be used.

Adaptations: Differentiated instruction, accommodations, and examples of adaptations. Discuss what you intend to do to support student learning as a whole class and as individuals. Be sure to make adaptations for different groups of students, too—plan to support the below-target group of students, the underperforming group of students, and the above-target group of students. State supports for individual students with an Individualized Education Plan (IEP), the 504, the English language learner (ELL), the underperforming, the struggling, and the gifted and talented. Broadly speaking, provide support where appropriate; for example:

- Use discussion starters, sentence frames, graphic organizers, models, demonstrations, scaffolding, so on.
- Define vocabulary using both an example and a counterexample. Some vocabulary terms in mathematics are used in common English but have a different meaning when used in a math class; for example, *difference*, *product*, and *volume*; thus, be explicit and distinguish how the terms are used in mathematics.
- Make considerations for instructional accommodations. Use *I do–we do–you do* approach, especially with primary elementary students, since the strategy is linear, not eclectic.
- Make considerations for assessment accommodations; for example, fewer problems for below-target students and challenging problems for above-target students.
- Remember for each lesson, specify exactly what the support is, in depth, with examples and valid reasoning:
  - ◊ I will give the ELL student the sentence frame, "The number 25 is ___ because ___" to justify their reasoning as to why it is a composite number." http://www.air.org/
  - ◊ I will display an anchor chart of vocabulary terms such as *factor* and *composite numbers*.
  - ◊ I will give a two-set Venn diagram graphic organizer for the gifted student to compare and contrast composite numbers versus odd numbers as the rest of the class works on defining composite numbers and listing all of them up to 50.

Respect students' cultural and diverse backgrounds while teaching them equitably and inclusively.

Instructional procedures should consist of intro-body-closure. Allot time and plan essential questions for each step:

(1) Introduction/time/questions (Bloom's): How long is this section? Things that can be done are to (a) pose questions to assess prior knowledge; (b) review past lessons; (c) state the expectations, objectives, and learning targets and state why the learning targets are important; and (d) hook and motivate by using history, personal interests, or community interests. Be sure to engage students and implement a transition technique to the main body of the lesson.

(2) Main body/time/questions (Bloom's): How long is this section? Differentiate instruction, incorporate a variety of assessments and classroom interactions, and execute the supports for diverse learners. Implement developmental activities:
   – If appropriate for this lesson model, check for understanding, do guided practice, do independent practice (*I do–we do–you do* or any variation of this).
   – Learning tasks should engage students, tying in prior knowledge, incorporate student interests, and deepen mathematical content.
   – Anticipate possible misconceptions, misunderstandings, errors, partial understandings, and preconceptions that might arise and plan for them.

(3) Closure/time/questions (Bloom's): How long is this section? Pose follow-up questions. What have you learned today? What questions do you still have? Actively engage the students in stating what they have learned in the lesson

Extension task: This is not homework, and it is not doing the same task targeted in the main body of the lesson. Plan an enrichment task aligned to the lesson's objectives. The teacher can also use the task with the whole class if the lesson is short and more time is still available for math. If this is not the case, then the task can be given to above-target students or the gifted and talented students. This is a great section to use children's literature or a scholarly website aligned to the objectives of the lesson.

Homeschool connections: State how the student's caregiver will be involved with the lesson or related homework, whether it be practice, supplemental work, or an enrichment task either manually or online.

Lesson plan sources: State sources of the ideas for the lesson, such as textbooks and websites used, plus the source of the lesson; for example, State Learning Standards for Mathematics.

See a sample lesson plan in the appendix "Wholes and Parts."

Digital Technology

Digital technologies can be used in different ways in teaching and learning mathematics, both inside and outside the classroom; for example, currently the *flipped classroom method* is gaining popularity. Dick and Hollebrands (2011) point out technologies that are used by students, such as Geogebra, iPad apps, calculators, TinkerPlots, and those used by teachers to teach or communicate math content, such as PowerPoint, videos, and Smart Boards.

The digital boards have mainly been used as "elevated" blackboards. The use of interactive whiteboards should go beyond using it as a blackboard or projector for various websites. By using Smart Notebook, many interactive slides can be developed. For example, when teaching place value, divisions for powers of 10 can be drawn. Circles representing units can be drawn. Students can circle groups of 10 and then, after removing the group, place a circle around the next power of 10.

Teachers can engage students in any part of the lesson, be it the introduction, main body, or closure, by using digital technologies; for example, the "poll everywhere" technique, using any device—smartphones, tablets, laptops, i-clickers, or any text-messaging device.

Calculators

Calculators can be used in mathematics as a tool for exploration and inquiry and much more. Calculators can be used to explore the prime factors of numbers, sequences, and sum of even and odd numbers. For example, students can investigate when two sequences have the same number and then generalize when this will happen for any two sequences. Students can also investigate maximum area possible with a certain perimeter or minimum area for a specific perimeter. In addition, students can find the number of exposed faces for a number of cubes as the cubes are formed into different rectangular solids.

Calculators can be used as an aid in computation or for checking accuracy of work. They can be used to help struggling students, such as allowing a student having difficulty carrying out multiplication in a problem-solving task where multiplication is not the focus of the task to use a calculator as an aid. The calculator removes the drudgery and unnecessary tedious work that takes the student's energy away from problem solving and investigation of mathematics.

Software

There are many software packages online or in DVDs that can be used in mathematics. They can be classified specifically as drill and practice, games, tutorial, tools, simulations, or problem-solving software, as well as a blend of two or more of these categories.

Drill-and-practice software reinforces learning of a skill. It gives practice for facts and skill that has been previously taught. Mainly this software offers independent tasks with the aim of achieving mastery. A question is presented to a student, who then answers before the answer is scored as correct or incorrect. These scores are saved for evaluation. Some forms of this type of software are able to differentiate the level of difficulty of the questions based on a student's response from easy to medium to challenging level or vice versa. The IXL (www.ixl.com/math/) provides such practice.

Games software is simply enhanced drill-and-practice software. These games are exciting, rewarding, and fun to work on since they are more flexible and allow for more than one strategy, as well as problem solving, creativity, and logical reasoning. At times a student pairs up with the computer, where the goal is mastery and subtle practice of skills, such as: http://www.mathplayground.com/.

Tutorial software tutors a student by exposition of new concept, fact, or skill before giving the student the opportunity to practice, such as: https://learnzillion.com/.

Simulation software permits students to explore and investigate tasks that are generally time consuming in an efficient manner. Students must apply, analyze, evaluate, and use critical thinking to carry out the learning task; for example: http://www.tinkerplots.com/.

Tools software comprises spreadsheets, interactive calculators, apps, and more, such as: https://sites.google.com/site/ti83interactivecalculator/Home.

Problem-solving software is a blend of other categories and employs no or minimal practice and drill. Students must manipulate all the times and problem solve. Examples are Geogebra (https://www.geogebra.org/), Gizmos (http://www.explorelearning.com/), and LOGO software, which has developmentally appropriate elementary computer programming language.

Generally, good software should be user-friendly, be visually attractive, capture a user's interest, provide feedback, be interactive, give quality instructional material, encourage higher and divergent thinking, support learning, and differentiate instruction.

Website

The World Wide Web has innumerable websites to visit that range from commercial to scholastic sites—the .com, .net, .org, and .edu. As a teacher it is important to pick scholarly websites for your own professional development, for your students, and for the parents of your students. Tread carefully when it comes to the dot-coms. Website resources for teacher candidates are plentiful:

(i)   You can use the NYS Testing site, http://www.nystce.nesinc.com/, for self-study. How? First find any grade 3 to 8 mathematical questions, then solve. Second, practice naming the mathematical understandings (concepts, facts, procedures, reasoning, and so on) embedded in this assessment, including both the Common Core content and practice standards. Finally, corroborate your answer to the task by checking your analysis using the provided annotated answer.

(ii) You can use the videos found on www.teachingchannel.org to scrutinize classroom instruction for best practices. This website contains sample lessons on a variety of mathematical topics at different grade levels.

(iii) The National Library of Virtual Manipulatives, http://nlvm.usu.edu/en/nav/vlibrary.html, has virtual manipulatives sorted by grade level and mathematical topic.

(iv) You can study the progression of K–6 mathematics content on this site: http://ime.math.arizona.edu/progressions/.

In concluding this section on tools and resources, we would like to point out that we are living in the sometimes overwhelming information age. Teacher candidates ought to know and ought to pick scholarly resources against commercially driven ones. They should be able to choose research-based resources that feature best practices. Additionally, effective teachers must be flexible to adapt to innovative and technological changes immediately and be updated on the best current resources that meet the needs of all students equitably.

TERMS TO PONDER

Realia	Flipped classroom	Digital technologies
Poll everywhere	Enrichment	Differentiated instruction
Adaptation	Anchor chart	Culturally responsive
Word wall	Task card	Learning target
Show me	Exit slip	Gifted and talented
Manipulative	Multiple strategies	Age appropriate
Motivation	Learning objective	Essential questions
Think aloud	Independent practice	Targeted teaching language

ACTIVITY 6.1: Find a math literature book and in one page, respond to the questions below.

1. Write the author, date, title, publisher, and ISBN of your book.
2. Why would you use this book to teach mathematics?
3. Name mathematics content domain and standard associated with this book by referring to the Core Curriculum standards. Give example from the reading to support the choice of standard.

ACTIVITY 6.2: Write at least three math-related questions that you would pose (verbal or written) to your students. Ensure the questions range in level of difficulty based on Bloom's taxonomy.

ACTIVITY 6.3: Define *manipulative, activity, worksheet,* and *game.*

ACTIVITY 6.4: Provide classroom scenarios where your role is that of an instructor, an observer, a facilitator, a coach, an actor, and a model.

ACTIVITY 6.5: Distinguish between prior knowledge, prerequisite knowledge, pretest, pre-assessment, posttest and post-assessment.

ACTIVITY 6.6: Annotated website review task:

- Locate on the Internet seven *exemplary* and *scholarly* educational sites. All sites must be related to elementary mathematics. Websites that offer *only flashcards and worksheets* will not have enough quality for this task and are not valued.
- Include for each site: the name of the site, the web address, when you visited, and a paragraph. The paragraph should describe the site and *why* it is valuable or worthwhile. You should support, *by example*, why the site is valuable or worthwhile. Just describing the content of the site is not enough. Focus on quality.
- Of the seven *different* sites:
  ◊ Two must be appropriate for *teachers.*
  ◊ Two must be appropriate for *students.*
  ◊ Two must be appropriate for *parents.*
  ◊ One must be a *virtual field trip.* This site must virtually "go" somewhere.

Websites

www.casio.com

Tools: This website provides information on various electronic tools that teachers can use to enhance student learning. Some of these tools include watches, projectors, digital cameras, keyboards, and calculators.

www.hand2mind.com

Tools: This website provides information on various tools and resources that teachers can use to improve their mathematics instruction. The tools available include activity books, manipulatives, calculators, rulers, and more. Additional resources provided by the website include professional development information, online resources, digital and multimedia options, and math games for students.

www.motionmathgames.com (apps)—*Students:* This website provides apps for fun and engaging math games for students at all grade levels.

www.amplify.com/math *Tools:* Early math assessment software in English and Spanish for grades K–3. This software poses questions to uncover students' mathematical reasoning and to measure fundamental skills required by the Common Core State Standards.

www.thinkthroughmath.com *Tools:* Think Through Math is a web-based solution that provides adaptive math instruction for students from grade 3 through Algebra 1. It is a program developed with the help of teachers and technologists to help students prepare for the Common Core standards and assessments.

www.successfulmathematics.com *Tools:* Teachers can use this site for math e-books for math 1, 2, and 3. Along with each math e-book comes an aligned Common Core standard, example problems, explanations for each problem, lesson plans, quizzes, and unit tests all aligned and connected with one another to address the specified math standard.

www.casioeducation.com *Tools:* This website provides options and purchasing information for various calculators that students can use for different difficulty levels and subjects of math. These calculators include basic, fraction and scientific, and graphing. Additional software and products are also available through the website, such as overhead projectors.

http://csdt.rpi.edu/ *Tools:* This website is dedicated to culturally situated design tools. The curriculum provided teaches students math and computing through culture. Many cultural designs are based on math and computing principles. This software will help students learn these principles as they simulate the original artifacts and develop their own creations.

Pre-K–6 Mathematics Content

Introduction

In this section we share selected pre-K–6 mathematics content and assessment from each domain, since it is not possible to cover all of it in this book. It is important to have mathematics content knowledge of a grade level above and a grade level below your targeted grade level math idea for a lesson. For instance, if planning to teach 2.OA.1, which is second grade's first standard on Operations and Algebraic Thinking, then you need to be aware of first-grade (1.OA) and third-grade (3.OA) standards on Operations and Algebraic Thinking. Similarly, you must be aware of 5.G standards and 7.G standards if you are to teach 6.G.1, even though you are not a certified seventh-grade teacher.

We have posed several questions in this section labeled as *Q1, Q2* and so on that we would like you to attempt.

Counting and Cardinality—CC

Table 7.1: Central Focus of CC Cluster

GRADE LEVEL	COUNTING AND CARDINALITY (CC)
PK	• Know number names and the count sequence. • Count to tell the number of objects. • Compare numbers.
K	• Know number names and the count sequence. • Count to tell the number of objects. • Compare numbers.
1, 2, 3, 4, 5, 6	None

Number Sense—How many? Which one? Cardinal, ordinal, quantifying, sequencing, ordering, comparing, one-to-one correspondence, subitizing, counting on, counting back, skip counting, place value.

Q.1 Draw a Venn diagram to show the relationship of natural numbers, whole numbers, integers, rational numbers, and real numbers.

Operations and Algebraic Thinking—OA

Table 7.2: Central Focus of OA Cluster

GRADE LEVEL	OPERATIONS AND ALGEBRAIC THINKING (OA)
PK	• Understand addition as adding to and understand subtraction as taking from. • Understand simple patterns.
K	• Understand addition as adding to and understand subtraction as taking from. • Understand simple patterns.
1	• Represent and solve problems involving addition and subtraction. • Understand and apply properties of operations and the relationship between addition and subtraction. • Add and subtract within 20. • Work with addition and subtraction equations.
2	• Represent and solve problems involving addition and subtraction. • Add and subtract within 20. • Work with equal groups of objects to gain foundations for multiplication.
3	• Represent and solve problems involving multiplication and division. • Understand properties of multiplication and the relationship between multiplication and division. • Multiply and divide within 100. • Solve problems involving the four operations and identify and explain patterns in arithmetic.
4	• Use the four operations with whole numbers to solve problems. • Gain familiarity with factors and multiples. • Generate and analyze patterns.
5	• Write and interpret numerical expressions. • Analyze patterns and relationships.
6	None

Q.2 How many leap years are there from 1966 through 2016? How many days are there from January 1, 1966, to December 31, 2016? Write your answers using scientific notation.

Q.3 A box weighs 950g when empty and can hold 55 dictionaries, where each dictionary has a mass, of 2kg 100g. Find the mass of the box filled with these dictionaries.

Measurement and Data—MD

Table 7.3: Central Focus of MD Cluster

Grade Level	Measurement and Data (MD)
PK	• Describe and compare measurable attributes. • Sort objects and count the number of objects in each category.
K	• Describe and compare measurable attributes. • Sort objects and count the number of objects in each category.
1	• Measure lengths indirectly and by iterating length units. • Tell and write time. • Represent and interpret data.
2	• Measure and estimate lengths in standard units. • Relate addition and subtraction to length. • Work with time and money. • Represent and interpret data.
3	• Solve problems involving measurement and estimation of intervals of time, liquid volumes, and masses of objects. • Represent and interpret data. • Geometric measurement: Understand concepts of area and relate area to multiplication and to addition. • Geometric measurement: Recognize perimeter as an attribute of plane figures and distinguish between linear and area measures.
4	• Solve problems involving measurement and conversion of measurements from a larger unit to a smaller unit. • Represent and interpret data. • Geometric measurement: Understand concepts of angle and measure angles.
5	• Convert like measurement units within a given measurement system. • Represent and interpret data. • Geometric measurement: Understand concepts of volume and relate volume to multiplication and to addition.
6	None

- Length Measuring using nonstandards units
  ◊ No GAPS
  ◊ No OVERLAPS
  ◊ End-to-end
- Perimeter and Circumference—measuring, counting, formula
- Area of Regular and Irregular Shapes—counting unit squares, formula

- Volume and Capacity of Regular and Irregular Objects—measuring, counting unit cubes, formula
- Masses—metric system
- Collect, Organize, and Intepret Data—table, dot plot, line plot

Q.4 So many units of measurement! Name 10. So many different attributes to measure! Name 10. So many units for the same attribute! For example, length can be in cm, m, mm, km, ft, miles, yds, dm, and so on. Which one is the appropriate unit for length? Can kg be used as a unit of length? How do you know what units of measure align with what attribute?

Q.5 Discuss how the *volume* of a box is different from the high *volume* of TV or music. Similarly, a *degree*! You earn a college *degree* when you graduate; when you measure temperature, you can use *degrees* Celsius or Fahrenheit or Kelvin; and you can measure an angle in *degrees* or use the radian measure!

Q.6

1. Draw a scaled picture graph and a scaled bar graph for the colored shapes in Figure 7.1. Compare and contrast these two graphs.

2a. Use a spreadsheet/Excel to draw a pie chart labeled by percentages and by color of the shapes in Figure 7.1.
2b. Write two conclusions that you can make from your graph.

Figure 7.1: Colored Shape

Q.7(i)

Table 7.4: Conversion of Units

FLIGHT DATA	METRIC SYSTEM	ENGLISH SYSTEM
Ground speed	695 km/h	? mph
Head wind	? km/h	125 mph
Outside temperature	-64^0 C	? ^{0}F
Altitude	? m	38,002 ft
Distance to destination	553 km	? miles
Distance from origin	? km	3,597 miles

Locate the appropriate measurements in Table 7.4 and use them to:

a) Find the missing (?) values to the nearest ones.

b) Find the total distance from origin to destination of the flight in km and in miles.

Q. 7(ii)

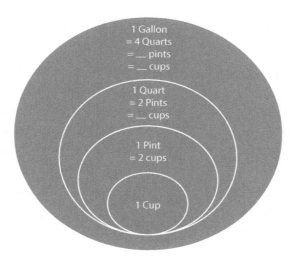

Number and Operations in Base Ten—NBT

Table 7.5: Central Focus of NBT Cluster

GRADE LEVEL	NUMBER AND OPERATIONS IN BASE TEN (NBT)
PK	None
K	• Work with numbers 11 to 19 to gain foundations for place value.
1	• Extend the counting sequence. • Understand place value. • Use place value understanding and properties of operations to add and subtract.
2	• Understand place value. • Use place value understanding and properties of operations to add and subtract.
3	• Use place value understanding and properties of operations to perform multi-digit arithmetic.
4	• Generalize place value understanding for multi-digit whole numbers. • Use place value understanding and properties of operations to perform multi-digit arithmetic.

(Continued)

GRADE LEVEL	NUMBER AND OPERATIONS IN BASE TEN (NBT)
5	• Understand the place value system. • Perform operations with multi-digit whole numbers and with decimals to hundredths.
6	None

- Addition
    - ◊ Combine, put together
    - ◊ Plus +
    - ◊ Addend + Addend = Sum
- Subtraction
    - ◊ Take away; comparison; missing-addend
    - ◊ Minus −
    - ◊ Minuend − Subtrahend = Difference
- Multiplication or "of"
    - ◊ Repeated addition; array—rectangular, dot, and so on
    - ◊ Equal groups—total, number of groups, and size of group
    - ◊ Times × or • or ( )
    - ◊ Factor × Factor = Product
- Division
    - ◊ Repeated subtraction; sharing; missing-factor
    - · ÷ or/or − (bar sign) or √ ("house")
    - ◊ Dividend ÷ Divisor = Quotient

Q.8

Arrange the stools in Figure 7.2 in as many different arrays as possible. Draw or sketch all of them. How many are there? How do you know you have all the possibilities?

Figure 7.2: Stools

Geometry—G

Table 7.6: Central Focus of G Cluster

GRADE LEVEL	GEOMETRY (G)
PK	• Identify and describe shapes (squares, circles, triangles, rectangles). • Analyze, compare, and sort objects.
K	• Identify and describe shapes. • Analyze, compare, and sort objects.
1	• Reason with shapes and their attributes.
2	• Reason with shapes and their attributes.
3	• Reason with shapes and their attributes.
4	• Draw and identify lines and angles, and classify shapes by properties of their lines and angles.
5	• Graph points on the coordinate plane to solve real-world and mathematical problems. • Classify two-dimensional figures into categories based on their properties.
6	• Solve real-world and mathematical problems involving area, surface area, and volume.

- Classifying, Sorting, Composing, and Decomposing shapes
- Spatial skills, Visualization skills, and Tessellation
- Similarity and Congruence
- Asymmetry and Symmetry—vertical, horizontal, or radial lines of symmetry
- Transformation—slide/translation; turn/rotation; flip/reflection; dilation/enlargement
- Angles—acute, right, obtuse, straight, reflex, and angle at a point
- Coordinate Geometry—maps, Cartesian graphs, graphs
- Nets and surface areas

Q.9 Draw an analog clock for each of the following: (a) the time you wake up, (b) 1:13 a.m., (c) your favorite time of the day, (d) 10:20 a.m., and (e) 7:45 p.m. Find the measure of the angle opening between the minute and hour hand for each of your clocks and also name the type of angle it is.

Statistics and Probability—SP

Table 7.7: Central Focus of SP Cluster

GRADE LEVEL	STATISTICS AND PROBABILITY (SP)
PK, K, 1, 2, 3, 4, 5	None
6	• Develop understanding of statistical variability. • Summarize and describe distribution.

Analyze data, using descriptive statistics

- Measures of center or central tendencies—mode, median, mean
- Measures of position—median, quartiles, deciles, percentiles
- Measures of spread or variability or dispersion—range, interquartile range, mean, absolute deviation

Graph—histograms, box plots—comparison of data

Numbers and Operations: Fractions—NF

Table 7.8: Central Focus of NF Cluster

GRADE LEVEL	NUMBER AND OPERATIONS: FRACTIONS (NF)
PK, K, 1, 2	None
3	• Develop understanding of fractions as numbers.
4	• Extend understanding of fraction equivalence and ordering. • Build fractions from unit fractions by applying and extending previous understandings of operations on whole numbers. • Understand decimal notation for fractions, and compare decimals.
5	• Use equivalent fractions as a strategy to add and subtract fractions. • Apply and extend previous understandings of multiplication and division to multiply and divide fractions.
6	None

- Fractions: Importance of the WHOLE; number line model; paper folding for notion of equivalence; area model for multiplication of a fraction by a fraction; How many groups of _____ (divisor) are in the _____ (dividend)?

- Decimal: Special fractions that represents subdivision of powers of tenths—tenths $\left(\dfrac{1}{10}\right)$, hundredths $\left(\dfrac{1}{100}\right)$, thousandths $\left(\dfrac{1}{1000}\right)$, and so on.

- Percent: A very special fraction; per hundred $\left(\dfrac{1}{100},\%\right)$.

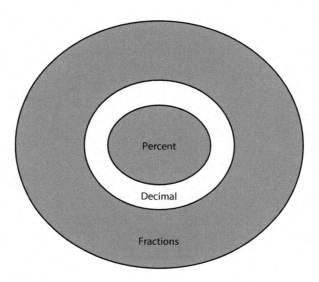

Q.10

A. Here is $\dfrac{3}{2}$ of a shape:

◊ Show how the **whole** shape might look.

◊ How might $\dfrac{1}{2}$ the shape look?

◊ Draw $\dfrac{3}{4}$ of this shape

◊ How might the TWO **wholes** look?

B. Here is $\frac{2}{3}$ of a group of small counters:

Show $\frac{3}{4}$ of the whole group.

Show the $1\frac{1}{3}$ group.

C. Here is $\frac{4}{3}$ of a strip of connecting cubes:

Show $2\frac{1}{3}$ of the whole group.

Expanding on the Rational Number System

Rational numbers are numbers that can be written in the form of $\frac{a}{b}$ where a, and b are integers, except b cannot be zero. Students have prior knowledge of parts of a whole and equivalent proportion; however, most of the strategies and set models they have used successfully with integers will not help them when using operations with fractions. We expand operation of rational numbers by using the measurement model.

Students need to have prior knowledge of graphing values on a number line. We propose that before performing operations using a number line, you should provide students opportunity to partition a whole into equal parts and label it.

1. The line below is a whole. Divide the whole into two equal parts and label each mark.

2. The line below is a whole. Divide the whole into five equal parts and label each mark.

3. The line below is a whole. Divide the whole into nine parts and label each mark.

Equivalent fractions can be explored on the number line in addition to using rectangle representation and manipulatives as a preliminary activity to operations with fractions. Equivalent fractions are a key concept when introducing operations with fractions. For example:

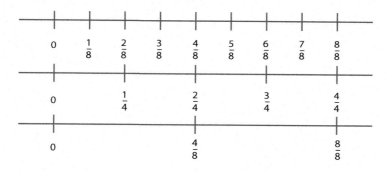

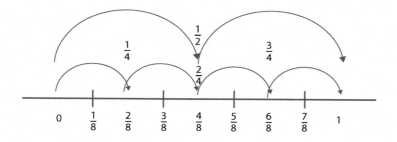

Therefore, $\frac{3}{8}$ and $\frac{1}{4}$ can be placed on the same scale if $\frac{1}{4}$ is changed to the equivalent fraction $\frac{2}{8}$. Fractions can be represented on the same number line if the scale is the same. The denominator denotes the scale. Finding the lowest common denominator can be delayed until students have a solid grasp of operations with fractions.

Addition

The problem: $\frac{1}{2} + \frac{1}{2}$, when placed on the number line, the answer is 1. Use of a number line easily helps counter students' misconception of adding the numerators together and the denominators together, which results in $\frac{2}{4}$ and simplifies to $\frac{1}{2}$. The problem can be confirmed with pattern blocks, partitioned (equal subdivisions) rectangles, or the number line. Solving same-denominator-fraction-addition problems in a variety of ways should confirm that addition of numerators results in a reasonable answer.

A partitioned rectangle is a better model to use for fractions than a circular model or pattern blocks. First, rectangles can be built with the x-tile from algebra tiles. For example $\frac{2}{5}$ uses five tiles with two of contrasting color to the other three, whereas $\frac{3}{4}$ uses four tiles where three have a contrasting color to the other one. Notice that there are different wholes, which is another reason for a common denominator.

Another reason common denominators are required for a fraction operation is that fractions can represent different sizes of wholes. The wholes have to be made the same for fraction operations to work. Equivalent fractions are the answer to making wholes the same.

A change of scale on the number line is required when fractions have different denominators. Knowing which fraction is larger at times helps when using the "adding on" strategy. Consider $\frac{1}{3} + \frac{5}{12}$:

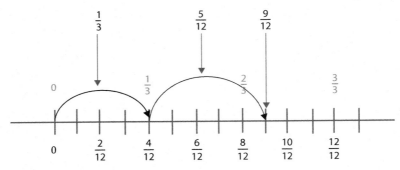

After drawing a number line with a scale of $\frac{1}{12}$s and placing $\frac{5}{12}$ on the number line, $\frac{1}{3}$ has an equivalent 12ths fraction. After counting out $\frac{4}{12}$ at the end of $\frac{5}{12}$, the answer of $\frac{9}{12}$ is obtained. An equivalent fraction for $\frac{9}{12}$ is $\frac{3}{4}$. For an example where the scale must be changed for both fractions $\frac{1}{4} + \frac{2}{3}$ can be tried.

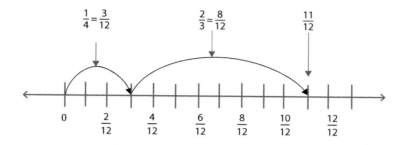

Here, $\frac{2}{3}$ was graphed first as the larger fraction. Multiplying the denominators together always gives a scale that can be used (always results in a denominator that allows the fractions to be added; $\frac{1}{4}$ is changed to its equivalent fraction, $\frac{3}{12}$.

Problem: $\frac{2}{5} + \frac{1}{4}$. A start is to use equivalent fractions to determine a scale. The same whole is needed to proceed—since both the denominator values divide 20 evenly, 20 is a good value to use because the number of scale markers is lowest (LCD). $\frac{8}{20} + \frac{5}{20}$. The units on the number line can be divided into 20ths. If both values are placed on the number line by "adding on," the answer is $\frac{13}{20}$. The solution can be confirmed on the number line, or manipulatives can be used for confirmation.

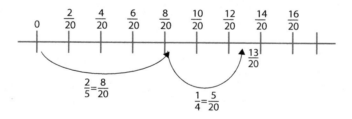

Using *tape diagrams* (visual) or *fraction bars* (manipulative) to solve $\frac{2}{5} + \frac{1}{4}$:

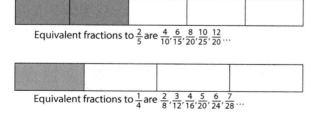

Equivalent fractions to $\frac{2}{5}$ are $\frac{4}{10}, \frac{6}{15}, \frac{8}{20}, \frac{10}{25}, \frac{12}{20} \cdots$

Equivalent fractions to $\frac{1}{4}$ are $\frac{2}{8}, \frac{3}{12}, \frac{4}{16}, \frac{5}{20}, \frac{6}{24}, \frac{7}{28} \cdots$

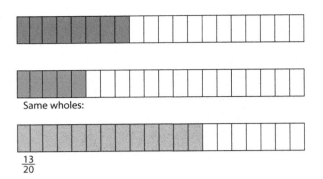

Same wholes:

$\frac{13}{20}$

Procedure of adding two unlike fractions vertically to a sum less than 1:

$\frac{2}{5} \qquad \rightarrow \frac{8}{20}$

$\frac{1}{4} \qquad \rightarrow \frac{5}{20} +$

$\qquad\qquad \frac{13}{20}$

As an introduction to mixed numbers, use fractions whose sum results in a number greater than 1, such as $\frac{2}{3} + \frac{3}{4}$.

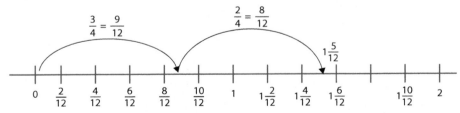

$\frac{2}{3} + \frac{3}{4} = \frac{8}{12} + \frac{9}{12} = \frac{17}{12}$ where $\frac{17}{12}$ can be decomposed into $1\frac{5}{12}$.

Vertical alignment of the procedure of addition of unlike fractions to a sum greater than 1:

$$\dfrac{2}{3} \qquad\qquad \dfrac{8}{12}$$

$$\dfrac{3}{4} \qquad + \dfrac{9}{12}$$

$$\dfrac{17}{12} \rightarrow \quad \dfrac{12}{12} + \dfrac{5}{12} = 1 + \dfrac{5}{12} = 1\,\dfrac{5}{12}$$

For mixed number addition, the whole number parts can be added, leaving the fractions to be dealt with in the preceding fashion. Why? This makes it less laborious. In using a number line, where the quantities are placed does not matter when you are adding; therefore, the whole parts can be done separately from the fractions.

Problem: $7\,\dfrac{7}{8} + 5\,\dfrac{2}{5}$

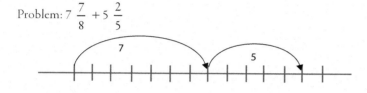

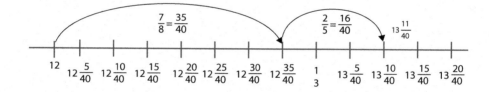

$$12 + \dfrac{2}{5} + \dfrac{7}{8} = 12 + \dfrac{16}{40} + \dfrac{35}{40} = 12 + \dfrac{51}{40} = 12 + 1 + \dfrac{11}{40} = 13 + \dfrac{11}{40} = 13\,\dfrac{11}{40}.$$

Vertical alignment of the procedure of adding two unlike mixed fractions:

$$5\,\dfrac{2}{5} \qquad \rightarrow 5\,\dfrac{16}{40}$$

$$7\,\dfrac{7}{8} \qquad \rightarrow 7\,\dfrac{35}{40} +$$

$$12\,\dfrac{51}{40} = 12 + 1 + \dfrac{11}{40} = 13 + \dfrac{11}{40} = 13\,\dfrac{11}{40}$$

Subtraction

Subtraction of fractions can be solved using the same strategy as addition. Revisit the number line and partitioned rectangles with appropriate values. Be careful not to create problems with negative answers.

Problem: $3\dfrac{5}{9} - 2\dfrac{3}{4}$

$$= 3\dfrac{5}{9} - 2\dfrac{3}{4} = 3\dfrac{20}{36} - 2\dfrac{27}{36}; \text{ a 1 needs to be unbundled from the 3;}$$

$$= 2\dfrac{36}{36} + \dfrac{20}{36} - 2\dfrac{27}{36}$$

$$= 2\dfrac{56}{36} - 2\dfrac{27}{36}$$

$$= \dfrac{29}{36}.$$

Vertical alignment of the procedure of subtracting two unlike mixed fractions:

$$3\dfrac{5}{9} \rightarrow 3\dfrac{20}{36} \rightarrow 2 + 1\dfrac{20}{36} \rightarrow 2 + \dfrac{36}{36} + \dfrac{20}{36} \rightarrow 2\dfrac{56}{36}$$

$$2\dfrac{3}{4} \rightarrow 2\dfrac{27}{36} \rightarrow 2\dfrac{27}{36} \rightarrow 2\dfrac{27}{36} \quad \rightarrow 2\dfrac{27}{36} \;-$$

$$\rule{5cm}{0.4pt}$$

$$\dfrac{29}{36}$$

$$3\dfrac{5}{9} - 2\dfrac{3}{4} = 1\dfrac{5}{9} - \dfrac{3}{4}$$

In the figure, $\frac{3}{4}\left(=\frac{27}{36}\right)$ cannot be subtracted from $\frac{5}{9}\left(=\frac{20}{36}\right)$. If the 1 from the whole number subtraction is graphed, the fraction subtraction can be completed without a negative result.

Multiplication

Scaling needs to be added to the concept of repeated addition for multiplication of fractions. Essentially, $\left(\frac{1}{2}\right)(24)$ reduces 24 to half of its size. In addition, 24 halves can be added to obtain 12. The procedure is relatively straightforward, but when proportions are introduced, students cross-multiply $\left(\frac{3}{4}\right)\left(\frac{5}{6}\right)$, forgetting that an equal sign is necessary. What students often lack is a conceptual understanding of what is actually taking place.

Address the misconception that "multiplication always results in a larger product." For example, $\left(\frac{1}{2}\right)\left(\frac{1}{2}\right)=\frac{1}{4}$.

Division

Division can be thought of in three different ways. First, measurement is a reason to use division. For example, if a sheet of fabric is 30 yards long, how many $1\frac{2}{3}$ yard pieces can be cut from the sheet? $\frac{30}{1\frac{2}{3}}=\frac{30}{\frac{5}{3}}=\frac{30}{\frac{5}{3}}=30\left(\frac{3}{5}\right)=18$ pieces.

Students should understand the concept behind the equivalence of dividing by a fraction and multiplying by its reciprocal.

$$\frac{30}{1\frac{2}{3}}=\frac{30}{\frac{5}{3}}=\frac{30}{\frac{5}{3}}\frac{\frac{3}{5}}{\frac{3}{5}}=\frac{30\left(\frac{3}{5}\right)}{1}=30\left(\frac{3}{5}\right)=18$$

Second, division can be used to determine the number of objects in a group. Students have the most experience with this type of problem. How many groups of 4 are in 12? $\frac{12}{4}$.

The experience students bring to this type of division problem calls for making the problem more difficult. For example, if $\frac{1}{8}$ kg tins are shipped in a box weighing 8 kg, how many packages of 5 tins can be made? $8\div\frac{5}{8}=\frac{64}{5}=12$ packages with 4 tins left over.

Third, division can be used to find factors. For example, if the area of a rectangle is $15\frac{1}{2}$ square meters and the length is $6\frac{1}{3}$ meters, what is the width of the rectangle?

$$15\frac{1}{2} = \left(6\frac{1}{3}\right)(\text{width}) \quad \text{dividing both sides of the equation by } 6\frac{1}{3} \text{ gives}$$

$$\left(15\frac{1}{2}\right) \div \left(6\frac{1}{3}\right) = \text{width}$$

$$\left(\frac{31}{2}\right) \div \left(\frac{19}{3}\right) = \left(\frac{31}{2}\right)\left(\frac{3}{19}\right) = \frac{93}{28}$$

$$\text{Width} = 3\frac{9}{28} \text{ meters}$$

The three ways of looking at division:

$6 \div 2$ Answers: three lengths of 2, two groups of 3, or 3 is the missing factor.

$4 \div \left(\frac{1}{2}\right)$ Answers: eight lengths of $\frac{1}{2}$, one half a group of 8, or 8 is the missing factor.

$\left(\frac{1}{4}\right) \div \left(\frac{1}{3}\right)$ Answers: Three quarters of a length of $\frac{1}{3}$, One third of a group of $\frac{3}{4}$, or $\frac{3}{4}$ is the missing factor. In this case, finding a common denominator for the dividend and the divisor makes what is happening clearer.

Three quarters of a length of $\frac{1}{3}$

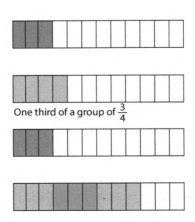

One third of a group of $\frac{3}{4}$

Missing factor ($\frac{1}{4} = \frac{1}{3} \times$ missing factor).

Change the problem to $\frac{1}{3} \div \frac{1}{4}$. Then $1\frac{1}{3}$ lengths of $\frac{1}{4}$ is the result.

Here is a final activity on this Number and Operations: Fractions (NF) domain. State the names of algorithms that you know of and illustrate each with an example, such as using a tape diagram to find the product of 6.47×63.

	X6 ONES	X4 TENTHS	X7 HUNDREDTHS
63	378 ones	252 tenths	441 hundredths
	378	25.2	4.41

Therefore, $6.47 \times 63 = 378 + 25.2 + 4.41 = 407.61$.

Ratios and Proportional Relationships—RP

Table 7.9: Central Focus of RP Cluster

GRADE LEVEL	RATIOS AND PROPORTIONAL RELATIONSHIPS (RP)
PK, K, 1, 2, 3, 4, 5	None
6	• Understand ratio concepts and use ratio reasoning to solve problems.

Q.11 (a) Draw an analog clock to show 11:10 a.m. Find the measure of the angle opening between the minute and hour hand. (b) Use ratio reasoning to find the length of the major arc given that the length of the minor arc formed in part (a) is 9.2cm.

Q.12 Students in a class of 21 were each given a mug with the school's logo on it as a gift. The teacher used 3 meters of ribbon to tie 5 of these gift boxes. How much ribbon is needed for the remaining gifts? If the cost of 1 meter of ribbon is 75 cents, how much did the teacher spend on the ribbon in dollars?

Q.13 The Empire State Building has a height of 1,454 feet and 102 stories. The 102nd floor is 1,250 feet high. The elevator in this building moves at 15mph; how long will it take to reach the 102nd floor? Assuming proportionality of the floors, how high is the 65th floor?

Q.14 Compare and contrast fraction, rate, ratio, unit rate, and percent.

Q.15 Four ninths of my lottery winnings goes for saving; one fifth of the remainder for shopping, and one fourth of what is left goes for charity. If $279 remains, what was the total lottery amount?

Expressions and Equations—EE

Table 7.10: Central Focus of EE Cluster

GRADE LEVEL	EXPRESSIONS AND EQUATIONS (EE)
PK, K, 1, 2, 3, 4, 5	None
6	• Apply and extend previous understandings of arithmetic to algebraic expressions. • Reason about and solve one-variable equations and inequalities. • Represent and analyze quantitative relationships between dependent and independent variables.

The Number System—NS

Table 7.11: Central Focus of NS Cluster

GRADE LEVEL	THE NUMBER SYSTEM (NS)
PK, K, 1, 2, 3, 4, 5	None
6	• Apply and extend previous understandings of multiplication and division to divide fractions by fractions. • Compute fluently with multidigit numbers and find common factors and multiples. • Apply and extend previous understandings of numbers to the system of rational numbers.

In conclusion to this section, we would like to point out that the breadth and depth of mathematical content knowledge enhances one's ability to teach mathematics effectively. The learning of this specialized content knowledge is continual and is an ongoing process. Keep learning!

TERMS TO PONDER

Subitize	Ratio reasoning	Tape diagrams
Rational numbers	Proportional reasoning	Mixed numbers
Measure of center	Patterns of learning	Variability
Equation	Statistical process	Real numbers
Integers	Array	Expression

Websites

www.qwizdom.com

Tools/Teachers: Qwizdom is a learning solution with software that provides an interactive and engaging mathematics curriculum, which helps increase participation, provide immediate data feedback, and most importantly, accelerate and improve comprehension and learning of K–12 students.

www.theOutstandingguides.com

Tool/Resource: This website provides information on the Outstanding Math Guide (OMG). The OMG is a tool/ resource that teachers and administrators can use to help students learn various math concepts throughout the year using creative graphic organizers, which contain steps, examples, and vocabulary for each concept students' encounter. There are OMG kits available for second grade through high school, and they cover all the topics in math that students will encounter in each specified grade.

Ball, D. L., Thames, M. H., & Phelps, G. (2008). Content knowledge for teaching: What makes it special? *Journal of Teacher Education, 59*, 389–407.

Barlow, A. T., & Harmon, S. (2012). CCSSM: Teaching 3 and 4. *Teaching Children Mathematics, 18*(8), 498–507.

Ben-Chaim, D., Keret, Y., & Ilany, B. (2012). *Ratio and proportion: Research and teaching in mathematics teachers' education*. Boston: Sense.

Bleiler, S. K., Baxter, W. A., Stephens, D. C., & Barlow, A. T. (2015). Constructing meaning: Standards for mathematical practice. *Teaching Children Mathematics, 21*(6), 336–344.

Bleiler, S. K., & Thompson, D. R. (2012). Multidimensional assessment of CCSSM. *Teaching Children Mathematics, 19*(5), 292–300.

Cai, J., Kaiser, G., Perry, B., & Wong, N. (Eds.) (2009). *Effective mathematics teaching from teachers' perspectives: National and cross-national studies*. Boston: Sense.

Calder, N. (2011). *Processing mathematics through digital technologies: The primary years*. Boston: Sense.

Chialvo, D., & Bak, P. (1999). Learning from mistakes. *Neuroscience, 90*(4), 1137–1148.

Chval, K., Lannin, J., & Jones, D. (2013). *Putting essential understanding of fractions into practice: 3–5* (K. Chval & B. J. Dougherty, Eds.). Reston, VA: National Council of Teachers of Mathematics (NCTM).

Common Core State Standards in Mathematics. (2010). Mathematics standards. Retrieved from http://www.corestandards.org/Math

Dacey, L., & Polly, D. (2012). CCSSM: The big picture. *Teaching Children Mathematics, 18*(6), 378–383.

Dick, T. P., & Hollebrands, K. F. (2011). *Focus in high school mathematics: Technology to support reasoning and sense making*. Reston, VA: NCTM.

Doering, A., & Veletsianos, G. (2009). Teaching with instructional software. In M. D. Roblyer & A. Doering (Eds.), *Integrating educational technology into teaching* (pp. 73–108). Upper Saddle River, NJ: Pearson Education.

Dreher, A., & Kuntze, S. (2015). Teacher's professional knowledge and noticing: The case of multiple representations in the mathematics classroom. *Educational Studies in Mathematics, 88*(1), 89–114.

Dweck, C. (2006). *Mindset: The new psychology of success*. New York: Random House.

edTPA. (2015). Elementary education handbook. Retrieved from http://edtpa.aacte.org

Engage New York (EngageNY.org). (n.d.). New York State math curriculum. Retrieved from https://www.engageny.org/mathematics

Ernst, K., & Ryan, S. (2014). *Success from the start: Your first years teaching elementary mathematics.* Reston, VA: NCTM.

Exemplars K–12. (n.d.). Mathematics K–6 common core-based assessment task; student's sample work; annotated student sample work (novice...expert). Retrieved from http://www.exemplars.com/education-materials/math-k-12

Gengiz, N. (2013). Facilitating productive discussions. *Teaching Children Mathematics, 19*(7), 450–456.

Islas, D. (2011). *How to assess while you teach: Formative assessment practices and lessons, grades K–2* (J. A. Cross, Ed.). Multimedia Professional Learning Resource. Sausalito, CA: Scholastic.

Jacobs, V. R., Lamb, L. L. C, & Philipp, R. A. (2010). Professional noticing of children's mathematical thinking. *Journal for Research in Mathematics Education, 41*(2), 169–202.

Kahneman, D. (2011). *Thinking, fast and slow.* New York: Farrar, Strauss, & Giroux.

Kastberg, S. E. (2014). Building mathematical practices: How many legs? *Teaching Children Mathematics, 20*(9), 538–540.

Lambdin, D. V., Kehle, P. E., & Preston, R. V. (1996). *Emphasis on assessment: Readings from NCTM's school-based journals.* Reston, VA: NCTM.

Lamberg, T. (2013). *Whole class mathematics discussions: Improving in-depth mathematical thinking and learning.* Boston: Pearson Education.

Mason, J., Burton, L., & Stacey, K. (2010). *Thinking mathematically.* Harlow, UK: Pearson Education.

Merriam Webster Dictionary http://www.merriam-webster.com/

Moser, J., Schroder, H., Heeter, C., Moran, T., & Lee, Y. (2011). Mind your errors: Evidence for a neural mechanism linking growth mindset to adaptive post-error adjustments. *Psychological Science, 22*(12), 1484–1489.

National Council of Teachers of Mathematics. (2014). *Principles to actions: Ensuring mathematics success for all.* Reston, VA: National Council of Teachers of Mathematics.

National Research Council. (2001). *Adding it up: Helping children learn mathematics* (J. Kilpatrick, J. Swafford, & B. Findell, Eds.). Mathematics Learning Study Committee. Center for Education, Division of Behavioral and Social sciences and Education. Washington, DC: National Academy Press.

New York State Department of Education. (2011). New York State P–12 Common Core learning standards for mathematics. Retrieved from http://www.p12.nysed.gov/ciai/common_core_standards/pdfdocs/nysp12cclsmath.pdf

New York State Teacher Certification Examinations (NYSTCE). (n.d.). edTPA for New York State. Retrieved from http://www.nystce.nesinc.com/NY_annTPA.asp

New York State Testing Program. (2012). Mathematics Common Core Sample questions. Grade 4 Mathematics.

Principles and Standards for School Mathematics. (2000). Reston, VA: National Council of Teachers of Mathematics.

Reys, R. E., Lindquist, M. M., Lambdin, D. V., & Smith, N. L. (2012). *Helping children learn mathematics* (10th ed.). Boston: Wiley.

Riccomini, P. J., & Witzel, B. S. (2010). *Response to intervention in mathematics.* Thousand Oaks, CA: Corwin-Sage.

Rigelman, N. (2011). Bring-do-leave: Nurturing reasoning and sense making. *Teaching Children Mathematics, 19*(7), 190–197.

Silbey, R. (2013). A closer look at mathematical practice 3: Explain and justify. *Teaching Children Mathematics, 20*(2), 70.

Skemp, R. (1976). Relational understanding and instrumental understanding. *Mathematics Teaching, 77,* 20–26.

Skemp, R. (2006). Relational understanding and instrumental understanding. *Mathematics Teaching in the Middle School, 12*(2), 88–95.

Van de Walle, J. A., Lovin, L. H., Karp, K. S., & Bay-Williams, J. (2014). Teaching student-centered mathematics: Developmentally appropriate instruction for grades Pre-K–2. Upper Saddle River, NJ: Pearson Education.

White, J., & Dauksas, L. (2012). CCSSM: Getting started K–grade 2. *Teaching Children Mathematics, 18*(7), 440–445.

Whote, D. Y., & Spitzer, J. S. (2009). *Mathematics for every student: Responding to diversity grades Pre-K–5* (C. E. Malloy, Ed.). Reston, VA: NCTM.

Xin, Y. P. (2012). *Conceptual model-based problem solving: Teach students with learning difficulties to solve math problems.* Boston: Sense.

Wholes and Parts—Sample Lesson Plan

Name: Sulwe Abaayo

Course & Block: EDUC 470:13

Lesson Plan Title: Wholes and Parts

Grade Level: 3

Class Description:

- The class is a heterogeneous class of 8 boys and 9 girls.
- Two students are classified as learning disabled in reading and written expression.
- One student is an English language learner.
- One student is classified as "gifted."
- One student is visually impaired.

Topic: Conceptualizing Fractions

NYCCS Standards:

- *Standard for Math Content 3.NF.1*

  Understand a fraction $1/b$ as the quantity formed by 1 part when a whole is partitioned into b equal parts; understand a fraction a/b as the quantity formed by a parts of size $1/b$.

- *Standard for Mathematical Practices:*

  1. Make sense of problems and persevere in solving them.

  5. Use appropriate tools strategically.

Learning Objectives:

- Student will be able to draw problems in handout 1 to represent a whole or a fractional part.
- Student will be able to solve problems in which a part is given by modeling the whole/part using geoboard, pattern blocks, snap cubes, and counters.

Materials:

- Plain paper, centimeter grid paper, geoboard, dot paper, Glue sticks, scissors.
- Pattern blocks, chips, or small counters, connecting cubes or snap cubes.
- Handout 1 at the end of lesson plan template (learning task with problems 1–5)
- Use of http://nlvm.usu.edu/ virtual manipulatives (e-manipulatives) for modeling examples and use Smart Board for reviewing lesson's content with the whole class.

Time Required: 1 hour

Targeted Vocabulary: Whole; Equal parts

Procedures:

Introduction: (10 minutes)

- State purpose of the lesson: "To investigate relationships between the whole and fractional parts using a variety of part/whole models." In this activity students start with parts of the whole and are asked to find the whole. For example, in order to interpret "one half," you have to know half of what? Half a page? Half the students in class today? Half the news time? Halftime in a Super Bowl game?
- Ask students to name a fractional portion of something and then find the whole: e.g., student can hold up their pencil and say here is 9/10 of a pencil; sketch the whole pencil. Listen to students' responses and examples of "half of _"; "here is 9/10," "find the whole," etc. (*Q & A assessment*)

Developmental Activity: (40 minutes)

- Give explicit directions on the task and ask student to restate— Point out materials for students to use; have students work in pairs; pass out handout 1 to partners (*written and show-me assessment—1st and 2nd objective respectively*)
- Allow students to have silent time to read the paper then to take a handful of materials; e.g., pattern blocks, etc.
- As students are working; circulate, observe, ask, and discuss with them. Ask different partners similar questions: (*Oral, verbally, observation, use of checklist assessment*)

◊ Which problems present the most difficulties? Why might that be? "How do you know?" "Show me."

◊ Are some fractions easier to work with? What fractions are easiest with pattern blocks, with geoboard, with snap cubes?

◊ As they finish their set of problems, suggest that they look over the whole set and discuss with others at their table how they did them, and look for strategies that work with all the problems. *Extension*: Partners then make up one problem for others to solve, formulating problems of their own using fractions. When complete, pairs should put their names on their problems and hand them to others at other tables to solve. Allow time for students to solve one another's problems. Point out that they must work through the invented problem to ensure that the problem is reasonable to solve.

Closure: (10 minutes)

- As a whole class review the activity by (1) Asking "what did you know about fractions that allowed you to solve the problems?" (2) Make a list of some of the ideas about fractions that students used to solve these problems.

- Anticipate possible answers, such as:

  ◊ Parts have to be equal. I know that $\frac{1}{6}$ is 1 of 6 equal parts.

  ◊ You can combine smaller parts to make bigger parts; e.g., $\frac{1}{6} + \frac{1}{6} + \frac{1}{6} = \frac{3}{6}$.

  ◊ Fractions bigger than one whole, have a larger numerator than the denominator.

Instructional/Environmental Modifications: (Adaptations for specific students)

- Two students are classified as learning disabled in reading and written expression. Read the problems aloud. Alternatively, reduce the number of problems to be solved and allow students to pick the hands-on material suitable for their needs.

- One student is an English language learner. Work one-on-one with this student; clarify directions using a step-by-step process and continually monitor progress, cueing student as needed.

- One student is visually impaired. The directions should be prepared in a larger font for this student.

- One student is classified as "gifted." During the developmental activity, this student's group should be encouraged to share their work. Also have ready extension problems for this student: (a) Student will write a fraction problem for peer to solve; (b) Using pattern blocks as hexagon cookies, write all the fractions that form the following:

  ◊ Different ways to make $\frac{5}{6}$

◊ Different ways to make 1 whole

◊ Different ways to make $\dfrac{5}{3}$

Home Connections/Outreach:

- Students will take their paper home and explain the class work to their families.
- Families will try to find one item at home, say, dry beans (set model) that can be used as materials to investigate the relationship between the whole and fractional parts.

Lesson Plan Source:

- New York State Common Core Curriculum State Standards in Mathematics (2011).
- Bridges to Classroom Mathematics (2003).
- http://nlvm.usu.edu/

1. Here is $\dfrac{1}{6}$ of a shape:
   Show how the whole shape might look:

2. Here is $\dfrac{3}{2}$ of a shape:

   How might $\dfrac{1}{4}$ the shape look?

3. The area of the figure drawn is half a fish:

   Sketch $\dfrac{1}{5}$ of the whole fish.

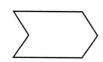

4. Here is $\dfrac{4}{5}$ of a group of smooth pebbles:

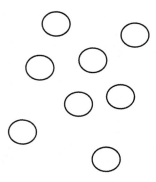

   Draw $2\dfrac{1}{2}$ of the smooth pebbles.

5. Here is $\dfrac{4}{3}$ of a strip of connecting cubes:

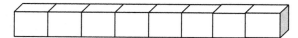

   Illustrate $\dfrac{2}{3}$ of the whole group:

Decimal Tests

Student 1

Round factors to estimate the product. Multiply.

1) 22 x 2.4

20 x 2 = 40

24 tenths
22
‾‾‾
48
48
‾‾‾
528 tenths

52.8 ones

2) 3.1 x 33

3 x 30 = 90

33
31 tenths
33
‾‾‾
99
99
‾‾‾
102.3 tenths

102.3 ones

3) 6.47 x 63

6 x 60 = 360

647 hundredths
63
‾‾‾
1941
3882
‾‾‾‾
407.61 hundredths

407.61 ones

4) 98 x 7.68

100 x 8 = 800

768 hundredths
98
‾‾‾
6144
6912
‾‾‾‾
75264 hundredths

752.64 ones

5) 83.41 x 504

500 x 80 = 40000

8341 hundredths
504
‾‾‾
33364
417050
‾‾‾‾‾
4203864 hundredths

42038.64 ones

6) 160.4 x 17

160 x 20 = 3200

1604 tenths
17
‾‾‾
11228
1604
‾‾‾‾
27268 tenths

2726.8 ones

7) Mr. Jansen is building an ice rink in his backyard that will measure 8.4 meters by 22 meters. What is the area of the rink?

84 tenths
22
‾‾‾
168
168
‾‾‾
1848 tenths

184.8 sq. meters

8) Rachel runs 3.2 miles each week day and 1.5 each day of the weekend. How many miles will she run in 6 weeks?

32 tenths
5
‾‾‾
160 tenths

15 tenths
2
‾‾‾
30 tenths

16 + 3 = 19 mi. in week

19
6
‾‾‾
114 miles

9) A slice of pizza costs $1.57. How much does 27 slices cost?

157 hundredths
27
‾‾‾
1099
314
‾‾‾
4239 hundredths

$42.39

10) A spool of ribbon holds 6.75 meters. If the craft club buys 21 spools what is the total cost of the ribbon selling for $2 per meter.

675 hundredths
21
‾‾‾
675
1350
‾‾‾‾
14175 hundredths

141.75

142
2
‾‾‾
$284

Student 2

Round factors to estimate the product. Multiply.

1) 22 x 2.4

  40

  52.8

2) 3.1 x 33

  90

  102.3

3) 6.47 x 63

  360

  407.61

4) 98 x 7.68

  800

  752.64

5) 83.41 x 504

  40000

  42038.64

6) 160.4 x 17

  3200

  2726.8

7) Mr. Jansen is building an ice rink in his backyard that will measure 8.4 meters by 22 meters. What is the area of the rink?

  184.8 m²

8) Rachel runs 3.2 miles each week day and 1.5 each day of the weekend. How many miles will she run in 6 weeks?

  114 miles

9) A slice of pizza costs $1.57. How much does 27 slices cost?

  $42.39

10) A spool of ribbon holds 6.75 meters. If the craft club buys 21 spools what is the total cost of the ribbon selling for $2 per meter.

  $284

Student 3

Round factors to estimate the product. Multiply.

1) 22 x 2.4

24 tenths
22
48
48
528 tenths

52.8 ones

2) 3.1 x 33

33
31 tenths
33
99
1023 tenths

102.3 ones

3) 6.47 x 63

647 hundredths
63
1941
3882
40761 hundredths

407.61 ones

4) 98 x 7.68

768 hundredths
98
6144
6912
75264 hundredths

752.64 ones

5) 83.41 x 504

8341 hundredths
504
33364
417050
4203864 hundredths

42038.64 ones

6) 160.4 x 17

1604 tenths
17
11228
1604
27268 tenths

2726.8 ones

7) Mr. Jansen is building an ice rink in his backyard that will measure 8.4 meters by 22 meters. What is the area of the rink?

84 tenths
22
168
168
1848 tenths   184.8 sq. meters

8) Rachel runs 3.2 miles each week day and 1.5 each day of the weekend. How many miles will she run in 6 weeks?

32 tenths
5
160 tenths

15 tenths
2
30 tenths

16
3
19 miles in a week

19
6
114 miles

9) A slice of pizza costs $1.57. How much does 27 slices cost?

157 hundredths
27
1099
314
4239 hundredths $42.39

10) A spool of ribbon holds 6.75 meters. If the craft club buys 21 spools what is the total cost of the ribbon selling for $2 per meter.

675 hundredths
21
675
1350
14175 hundredths

141.75 meters

142
2
$ 284

Student 4

Round factors to estimate the product. Multiply.

1) 22 x 2.4

2.0×2=40

24 tenths

22

48
48
---
528 tenths

52.8 ones

2) 3.1 x 33

3×30=90

33
31 tenths

33
99

1023 tenths

102.3 ones

3) 6.47 x 63

6×60=360

647 hundredths
63

1841
3771

39551 hundredths

395.51 ones

4) 98 x 7.68

100 × 8 = 800

768 hundredths
98

6114
6903

73144 hundredths

731.44 ones

5) 83.41 x 504

500×80 = 4000

8341 hundredths
504

33364
41705

4504140 hundredths

4504.140 ones

6) 160.4 x 17

160×20 = 32

1604 tenths
17

11128
1604

27168 tenths

2746.8 ones

7) Mr. Jansen is building an ice rink in his backyard that will measure 8.4 meters by 22 meters. What is the area of the rink?

84 tenths
22

168
168

1848 tenths

184.8 sq. meters

8) Rachel runs 3.2 miles each week day and 1.5 each day of the weekend. How many miles will she run in 6 weeks?

32 tenths
5
---
160 tenths

15 tenths
2
---
30 tenths

16
3
---
19 miles in a week

19
6
---
114 miles

9) A slice of pizza costs $1.57. How much does 27 slices cost?

157 hundredths
27

1098
314

4238 hundredths $42.38

10) A spool of ribbon holds 6.75 meters. If the craft club buys 21 spools what is the total cost of the ribbon selling for $2 per meter.

675 hundredths
21

675
1350

2025 hundredths

2.0.25

21
2

$42

Student 5

Round factors to estimate the product. Multiply.

1) 22 x 2.4

```
  24
  22
  48
 48
 52.8
```

2) 3.1 x 33

```
  33
  31
  33
  99
 1023
```

3) 6.47 x 63

```
  647
   63
 1941
 3882
 4076.10
```

4) 98 x 7.68

```
  768
   98
 6144
 6912
 75264.0
```

5) 83.41 x 504

```
  8341
   504
 33364
 417050
 4203864.0
```

6) 160.4 x 17

```
  1604
    17
 11228
 1604
 2726.8
```

7) Mr. Jansen is building an ice rink in his backyard that will measure 8.4 meters by 22 meters. What is the area of the rink?

```
  84
  22
 168
168
```
184.8 sq. m.

8) Rachel runs 3.2 miles each week day and 1.5 each day of the weekend. How many miles will she run in 6 weeks?

```
 32      15      16      19
  5       2       3       6
16.0     3.0     19     114 miles
```

9) A slice of pizza costs $1.57. How much does 27 slices cost?

```
 157
  27
1099
314
```
$423.90

10) A spool of ribbon holds 6.75 meters. If the craft club buys 21 spools what is the total cost of the ribbon selling for $2 per meter.

Student 6

Round factors to estimate the product. Multiply.

1) 22 x 2.4

```
    24
    22
  ----
    48
    48
  ----
   528
```

2) 3.1 x 33

```
    33
    31
  ----
    33
    99
  ----
  1023
```

3) 6.47 x 63

```
   647
    63
  ----
  1941
  3882
  ----
  40761
```

4) 98 x 7.68

```
   768
    98
  ----
  6144
  6912
  ----
  75264
```

5) 83.41 x 504

```
   8341
    504
  ----
  33364
  41705
  ----
  450414
```

6) 160.4 x 17

```
   1604
     17
  ----
  11228
  1604
  ----
  27268
```

7) Mr. Jansen is building an ice rink in his backyard that will measure 8.4 meters by 22 meters. What is the area of the rink?

```
    84
    22
  ----
   168
   168
  ----
```
1848

8) Rachel runs 3.2 miles each week day and 1.5 each day of the weekend. How many miles will she run in 6 weeks?

9) A slice of pizza costs $1.57. How much does 27 slices cost?

```
   157
    27
  ----
  1099
  314
```
4239

10) A spool of ribbon holds 6.75 meters. If the craft club buys 21 spools what is the total cost of the ribbon selling for $2 per meter.

Student 7

Round factors to estimate the product. Multiply.

1) 22 x 2.4

24 tenths
22
48
48
528 tenths   52.8 ones

2) 3.1 x 33

33
31 tenths
33
99
1023 tenths   102.3 ones

3) 6.47 x 63

4) 98 x 7.68

5) 83.41 x 504

6) 160.4 x 17

1604 tenths
17
11 228
1604
27268 tenths   2726.8 ones

7) Mr. Jansen is building an ice rink in his backyard that will measure 8.4 meters by 22 meters. What is the area of the rink?

84 tenths
22
168
168
          1848 tenths   184.8 sq. m.

8) Rachel runs 3.2 miles each week day and 1.5 each day of the weekend. How many miles will she run in 6 weeks?

32 tenths
5
160 tenths

15 tenths
2
30 tenths

16
3
19 days

19
144 days

9) A slice of pizza costs $1.57. How much does 27 slices cost?

10) A spool of ribbon holds 6.75 meters. If the craft club buys 21 spools what is the total cost of the ribbon selling for $2 per meter.

Student 8

Round factors to estimate the product. Multiply.

1) 22 x 2.4

20×2=40

24 tenths

22
48
48
528 tenths   528 ones

2) 3.1 x 33

3×30=90

33
31 tenths
33
99
1023 tenths   102.3 ones

3) 6.47 x 63   6×60 =360

647 hundredths
63
1841
3888
40721 hundredths   407.21 ones

4) 98 x 7.68   100×8=800

768 hundredths
98
5904
6612
72024 hundredths   720.24 ones

5) 83.41 x 504   500×80=40000

8341 hundredths
504
29864
417050
4464414 hundredths   4464.14 ones

6) 160.4 x 17   160 ×20=3200

1604 tenths
17
7448
1064
18088 tenths   1808.8 ones

7) Mr. Jansen is building an ice rink in his backyard that will measure 8.4 meters by 22 meters. What is the area of the rink?

84 tenths
22
168
168
1848 tenths   184.8 meters^2

8) Rachel runs 3.2 miles each week day and 1.5 each day of the weekend. How many miles will she run in 6 weeks?

32 tenths   15 tenths   16   19
5   2   3   6
160   30   19   114 miles
8 tenths 5   miles

9) A slice of pizza costs $1.57. How much does 27 slices cost?

157 hundredths
27
1089
314
4239 hundredths $42.39

10) A spool of ribbon holds 6.75 meters. If the craft club buys 21 spools what is the total cost of the ribbon selling for $2 per meter.

675 hundredths
21
675
1350
14175 hundredths   141.75   142
2
$284

Student 9

Round factors to estimate the product. Multiply.

1) 22 x 2.4

2.4 tenths
 22
___
 48   5.28 ones
 48
___
52.8 tenths

2) 3.1 x 33

  33
3.1 tenths
___
  33   1.023 ones
  99
___
1023 tenths

3) 6.47 x 63

6.47 hundredths
  63
___
1941   40.761 ones
3882
___
40761 hundredths

4) 98 x 7.68

7.68 hundredths
  98
___
6144   75.264 ones
6912
___
75264 hundredths

5) 83.41 x 504

8341 hundredths
  504
___
33364   42.03864 ones
417050
___
4203864 hundredths

6) 160.4 x 17

1604 tenths
  17
___
11228   2.7268 ones
1604
___
2.7268 tenths

7) Mr. Jansen is building an ice rink in his backyard that will measure 8.4 meters by 22 meters. What is the area of the rink?

8.4 tenths
  22
___
168   1.848 sq. m.
168
___
1848 tenths

8) Rachel runs 3.2 miles each week day and 1.5 each day of the weekend. How many miles will she run in 6 weeks?

3.2 tenths   1.5 tenths   1.6   4.6 tenths
  5   2   3   6   2.76 miles
___   ___   ___   ___
16.0 tenths   30 tenths   4.6 miles 27.6 tenths

9) A slice of pizza costs $1.57. How much does 27 slices cost?

1.57 hundredths
  27
___
1099   4239 hundredths $42.39
314

10) A spool of ribbon holds 6.75 meters. If the craft club buys 21 spools what is the total cost of the ribbon selling for $2 per meter.

6.75 hundredths   14.175   14
  21   2
___   ___
675                               $28
1350
___
14175 hundredths

Student 10

Round factors to estimate the product. Multiply.

1) 22 x 2.4

20 x 2 = 40

24 tenths
22
48   52.8 ones
48
528 tenths

2) 3.1 x 33

3 x 30 = 90

33
31 tenths
33   102.3 ones
99
1023 tenths

3) 6.47 x 63

6 x 60 = 360

647 hundredths
63   407.61 ones
1941
3882
40761 hundredths

4) 98 x 7.68

100 x 8 = 800

768 hundredths
98   752.64 ones
6144
6912
75264 hundredths

5) 83.41 x 504

500 x 80 = 40000

8341 hundredths
504   42038.64 ones
33364
417050
4203864 hundredths

6) 160.4 x 17

160 x 20 = 3200

1604 tenths
17   2726.8 ones
11228
1604
27268 tenths

7) Mr. Jansen is building an ice rink in his backyard that will measure 8.4 meters by 22 meters. What is the area of the rink?

84 tenths
22
168   1848 tenths   184.8 sq. meters
168

8) Rachel runs 3.2 miles each week day and 1.5 each day of the weekend. How many miles will she run in 6 weeks?

3.2 tenths   1.5 tenths   16 + 3 = 19 mi./week
5   2
160 tenths   30 tenths   19
                                          6
                                    114 miles

9) A slice of pizza costs $1.57. How much does 27 slices cost?

157 tenths
27   4239 tenths $42.39
1099
314

10) A spool of ribbon holds 6.75 meters. If the craft club buys 21 spools what is the total cost of the ribbon selling for $2 per meter.

675 tenths   141.75   142 meters
21   2
675                          $284
1350
14175 tenths

Student 11

Round factors to estimate the product. Multiply.

1) 22 x 2.4

$20 \times 2 = 40$

2) 3.1 x 33

$3 \times 30 = 90$

3) 6.47 x 63

$6 \times 60 = 360$

4) 98 x 7.68

$100 \times 8 = 800$

5) 83.41 x 504

$500 \times 80 = 40000$

6) 160.4 x 17

$160 \times 20 = 3200$

7) Mr. Jansen is building an ice rink in his backyard that will measure 8.4 meters by 22 meters. What is the area of the rink?

8.4
2.2
168
168

184.8 sq. m

8) Rachel runs 3.2 miles each week day and 1.5 each day of the weekend. How many miles will she run in 6 weeks?

3.2
5
16.0

1.5
2
3.0

16
3
19 miles

19
6
114 miles in 6 weeks

9) A slice of pizza costs $1.57. How much does 27 slices cost?

1.57
27
1099
314

$42.39

10) A spool of ribbon holds 6.75 meters. If the craft club buys 21 spools what is the total cost of the ribbon selling for $2 per meter.

6.75
21
675
1350
141.75

141.75
2
$283.50

Student 12

Round factors to estimate the product. Multiply.

1) 22 x 2.4

$$\begin{array}{r} 24 \\ 22 \\ \hline 48 \\ 48 \\ \hline 5280 \end{array}$$

2) 3.1 x 33

$$\begin{array}{r} 33 \\ 31 \\ \hline 33 \\ 99 \\ \hline 10230 \end{array}$$

3) 6.47 x 63

$$\begin{array}{r} 647 \\ 63 \\ \hline 1941 \\ 3882 \\ \hline 407610\,0 \end{array}$$

4) 98 x 7.68

$$\begin{array}{r} 768 \\ 98 \\ \hline 6144 \\ 6912 \\ \hline 752640\,0 \end{array}$$

5) 83.41 x 504

$$\begin{array}{r} 8341 \\ 504 \\ \hline 33364 \\ 417050 \\ \hline 4203864\,00 \end{array}$$

6) 160.4 x 17

$$\begin{array}{r} 1604 \\ 17 \\ \hline 11228 \\ 1604 \\ \hline 27268\,0 \end{array}$$

7) Mr. Jansen is building an ice rink in his backyard that will measure 8.4 meters by 22 meters. What is the area of the rink?

$$\begin{array}{r} 84 \\ 22 \\ \hline 168 \\ 168 \\ \hline 18480 \end{array}$$ 18480 m²

8) Rachel runs 3.2 miles each week day and 1.5 each day of the weekend. How many miles will she run in 6 weeks?

$$\begin{array}{r} 32 \\ 5 \\ \hline 1600 \end{array} \quad \begin{array}{r} 15 \\ 2 \\ \hline 300 \end{array} \quad \begin{array}{r} 1600 \\ 300 \\ \hline 1900 \end{array} \quad \begin{array}{r} 1900 \\ 6 \\ \hline 11400 \end{array}$$

9) A slice of pizza costs $1.57. How much does 27 slices cost?

$$\begin{array}{r} 157 \\ 27 \\ \hline 1099 \\ 314 \end{array}$$ $423900

10) A spool of ribbon holds 6.75 meters. If the craft club buys 21 spools what is the total cost of the ribbon selling for $2 per meter.

$$\begin{array}{r} 675 \\ 21 \\ \hline 675 \\ 1350 \\ \hline 1417500 \end{array} \quad \begin{array}{r} 1417500 \\ 2 \\ \hline 2835000 \end{array}$$

Student 13

Round factors to estimate the product. Multiply.

1) 22 x 2.4

```
   24
   22
   48
  48.
  52.8
```

2) 3.1 x 33

```
   33
   31
   33
   99
  102.3
```

3) 6.47 x 63

```
   647
    63
  1941
  3882
  3901.41
```

4) 98 x 7.68

```
   768
    98
  6144
 6912
 6973.44
```

5) 83.41 x 504

```
   8341
    504
   33364
  417050
  42038.64
```

6) 160.4 x 17

```
   1604
     17
   1122.8
   1604
   2726.8
```

7) Mr. Jansen is building an ice rink in his backyard that will measure 8.4 meters by 22 meters. What is the area of the rink?

```
   84
   22
  16.8
  168
 184.8  sq. m.
```

8) Rachel runs 3.2 miles each week day and 1.5 each day of the weekend. How many miles will she run in 6 weeks?

```
  32      15      16      19
   5       2       3       6
 16.0    3.0      19     114  miles
```

9) A slice of pizza costs $1.57. How much does 27 slices cost?

```
  157
   27
 1099     $ 324.99
314
```

10) A spool of ribbon holds 6.75 meters. If the craft club buys 21 spools what is the total cost of the ribbon selling for $2 per meter.

```
  675
   21
  675      142
 1350       2
 141.75    $ 284
```

Student 14

Round factors to estimate the product. Multiply.

1) 22 x 2.4

$$\begin{array}{r} 2.4 \\ 22. \\ \hline 48 \\ 48 \\ \hline 52.8 \end{array}$$

2) 3.1 x 33

$$\begin{array}{r} 33 \\ 31 \\ \hline 33 \\ 99 \\ \hline 102.3 \end{array}$$

3) 6.47 x 63

$$\begin{array}{r} 647 \\ 63 \\ \hline 1941 \\ 3882 \\ \hline 4076.1 \end{array}$$

4) 98 x 7.68

$$\begin{array}{r} 768 \\ 98. \\ \hline 6144 \\ 6912 \\ \hline 752.64 \end{array}$$

5) 83.41 x 504

$$\begin{array}{r} 8341 \\ 504 \\ \hline 33364 \\ 417050 \\ \hline 420386.4 \end{array}$$

6) 160.4 x 17

$$\begin{array}{r} 1604 \\ 17 \\ \hline 11228 \\ 1604 \\ \hline 2726.8 \end{array}$$

7) Mr. Jansen is building an ice rink in his backyard that will measure 8.4 meters by 22 meters. What is the area of the rink?

$$\begin{array}{r} 84 \\ 22 \\ \hline 168 \\ 168 \\ \hline 184.8 \end{array}$$ sq. m

8) Rachel runs 3.2 miles each week day and 1.5 each day of the weekend. How many miles will she run in 6 weeks?

$$\begin{array}{r} 32 \\ 5 \\ \hline 16.0 \end{array}$$ $$\begin{array}{r} 15 \\ 2 \\ \hline 3.0 \end{array}$$ $$\begin{array}{r} 16 \\ 3 \\ \hline 19 \end{array}$$ $$\begin{array}{r} 19 \\ 6 \\ \hline 114 \end{array}$$ miles

9) A slice of pizza costs $1.57. How much does 27 slices cost?

$$\begin{array}{r} 157 \\ 27 \\ \hline 1099 \\ 314 \end{array}$$ $42.39

10) A spool of ribbon holds 6.75 meters. If the craft club buys 21 spools what is the total cost of the ribbon selling for $2 per meter.

$$\begin{array}{r} 675 \\ 21 \\ \hline 675 \\ 1350 \\ \hline 1417.5 \end{array}$$ $$\begin{array}{r} 1418 \\ 2 \\ \hline \end{array}$$ $2836

Student 15

Round factors to estimate the product. Multiply.

1) 22 x 2.4

24 tenths
22
———
48
48
———
528 tenths

52.8 ones

2) 3.1 x 33

33
31 tenths
———
33
99
———
1023 tenths

102.3 ones

3) 6.47 x 63

647 hundredths
63
———
1941
3882
———
40761 hundredths

407.61 ones

4) 98 x 7.68

768 hundredths
98
———
6144
6912
———
75264 hundredths

752.64 ones

5) 83.41 x 504

8341 hundredths
504
———
33364
417050
———
4203864 hundredths

42038.64 ones

6) 160.4 x 17

1604 tenths
17
———
11228
1604
———
27268 tenths

2726.8 ones

7) Mr. Jansen is building an ice rink in his backyard that will measure 8.4 meters by 22 meters. What is the area of the rink?

84 tenths
22
———
168
168
———

1848 tenths

184.8 sq. meters

8) Rachel runs 3.2 miles each week day and 1.5 each day of the weekend. How many miles will she run in 6 weeks?

32 tenths
5
———
160 tenths

15 tenths
2
———
30 tenths

16
3
———
19 miles in a week

19
6
———
114 miles

9) A slice of pizza costs $1.57. How much does 27 slices cost?

157 hundredths
27
———
1099
314
———

4239 hundredths

$42.39

10) A spool of ribbon holds 6.75 meters. If the craft club buys 21 spools what is the total cost of the ribbon selling for $2 per meter.

675 hundredths
21
———
675
1350
———
14175 hundredths

141.75 meters

142
2
———
$284

Student 16

Round factors to estimate the product. Multiply.

1) 22 x 2.4

20 x 2 = 40

24 tenths
22.
48
48
96 tenths   9.6 ones

2) 3.1 x 33

3 x 30 = 90

33
31 tenths
33
99
132 tenths   13.2 ones

3) 6.47 x 63   6 x 60 = 360

647 hundredths
63
1941
3882
5823 hundredths   58.23 ones

4) 98 x 7.68   100 x 8 = 800

768 hundredths
98
6144
6912
13056 hundredths   130.56 ones

5) 83.41 x 504   500 x 80 = 40000

8341 hundredths
504
33364
417050
450414 hundredths   4504.14 ones

6) 160.4 x 17   160 x 20 = 3200

1604 tenths
17
11228
1604
12832 tenths   1283.2 ones

7) Mr. Jansen is building an ice rink in his backyard that will measure 8.4 meters by 22 meters. What is the area of the rink?

84 tenths
22
168
168
336 tenths   33.6 sq. m.

8) Rachel runs 3.2 miles each week day and 1.5 each day of the weekend. How many miles will she run in 6 weeks?

32 tenths   15 tenths   16   19
5   2   3   6
160 tenths   30 tenths   19 miles   114 total miles

9) A slice of pizza costs $1.57. How much does 27 slices cost?

157 hundredths
27
1099
314
1413 hundredths   14.13 dollars

10) A spool of ribbon holds 6.75 meters. If the craft club buys 21 spools what is the total cost of the ribbon selling for $2 per meter.

675 hundredths
21
675
1350
2025 hundredths   20.25   21
                                        2
                                        $42

Student 17

Round factors to estimate the product. Multiply.

1) 22 x 2.4

20 x 2 = 48
24 tenths
22
48   5280 ones
48
528 tenths

2) 3.1 x 33

33
31 tenths
33   102.3 ones
99
1023 tenths

3) 6.47 x 63

60 x 6 = 360
674 hundredths
63
2022   424.62
4044
424 62 hundredths

4) 98 x 7.68

768 hundredths
98
6144   752.64 ones
6912
752 64 hundredths

5) 83.41 x 504

8341 hundredths
504
33364   4504.14 ones
41705
45 0414 hundredths

6) 160.4 x 17

160 x 20 = 3200
1604 tenths
20
32 80 tenths   328.0 ones

7) Mr. Jansen is building an ice rink in his backyard that will measure 8.4 meters by 22 meters. What is the area of the rink?

84
22
168
168
1848   184.8 sq meters

8) Rachel runs 3.2 miles each week day and 1.5 each day of the weekend. How many miles will she run in 6 weeks?

32
5
16.0

15
2
3.0

16
3
18

19
6
114 days

9) A slice of pizza costs $1.57. How much does 27 slices cost?

157
27
1099 $42.39
314

10) A spool of ribbon holds 6.75 meters. If the craft club buys 21 spools what is the total cost of the ribbon selling for $2 per meter.

21
7
147

147
2
$294

Student 18

Round factors to estimate the product. Multiply.

1) 22 x 2.4

24 tenths
22
‾‾‾‾‾
48
48
‾‾‾‾‾
528 tenths

52.8 ones

2) 3.1 x 33

33
31 tenths
‾‾‾‾‾
93
99
‾‾‾‾‾
1023 tenths

102.3 ones

3) 6.47 x 63

647 hundredths
63
‾‾‾‾‾
1941
3882
‾‾‾‾‾
40761 hundredths

407.61 ones

4) 98 x 7.68

768 hundredths
98
‾‾‾‾‾
6144
6912
‾‾‾‾‾
75264 hundredths

752.64 ones

5) 83.41 x 504

8341 hundredths
504
‾‾‾‾‾
33364
417050
‾‾‾‾‾
4203864 hundredths

42038.64 ones

6) 160.4 x 17

1604 tenths
17
‾‾‾‾‾
11228
1604
‾‾‾‾‾
27268 hundredths

2726.8 ones

7) Mr. Jansen is building an ice rink in his backyard that will measure 8.4 meters by 22 meters. What is the area of the rink?

24 tenths
22
‾‾‾‾‾
168
168
‾‾‾‾‾
1848 tenths

184.8 sq. meters

8) Rachel runs 3.2 miles each week day and 1.5 each day of the weekend. How many miles will she run in 6 weeks?

32 tenths   15 tenths
5   2
‾‾‾‾‾   ‾‾‾‾‾
160 tenths   30 tenths

16
3
‾‾‾‾‾
19 miles in a week

19
6
‾‾‾‾‾
114 miles

9) A slice of pizza costs $1.57. How much does 27 slices cost?

157 hundredths
27   4239 hundredths
‾‾‾‾‾
1099 $42.39
314

10) A spool of ribbon holds 6.75 meters. If the craft club buys 21 spools what is the total cost of the ribbon selling for $2 per meter.

675 hundredths
21
‾‾‾‾‾
675
1350
‾‾‾‾‾
14175 hundredths

141.75 meters

142
2
‾‾‾‾‾
$ 284

Student 19

Round factors to estimate the product. Multiply.

1) 22 x 2.4

40

52.8

2) 3.1 x 33

90

102.3

3) 6.47 x 63

360

457.61

4) 98 x 7.68

800

752.64

5) 83.41 x 504

40000

42,038.64

6) 160.4 x 17

3200

2726.8

7) Mr. Jansen is building an ice rink in his backyard that will measure 8.4 meters by 22 meters. What is the area of the rink?

184.8 sq. meters

8) Rachel runs 3.2 miles each week day and 1.5 each day of the weekend. How many miles will she run in 6 weeks?

114 miles

9) A slice of pizza costs $1.57. How much does 27 slices cost?

$42.39

10) A spool of ribbon holds 6.75 meters. If the craft club buys 21 spools what is the total cost of the ribbon selling for $2 per meter.

$284

Student 2.0

Round factors to estimate the product. Multiply.

1) 22 x 2.4

20 x 2 = 40
24 tenths
22
48
48
528 tenths   52.8

2) 3.1 x 33

3 x 30 = 90
33
31 tenths
33
99
1023 tenths   102.3

3) 6.47 x 63   6 x 60 = 360

647 h
63
1941
3884
40781 h   407.81

4) 98 x 7.68

100 x 8
800

768 h
89
6912   683.52
6144
68352 h

5) 83.41 x 504

8341 h
504
33364   4238.64
417050
4238644 h

800 x 80 = 40000

6) 160.4 x 17   160 x 20 = 3200

1604 tenths
17
11428
1604
27468 tenths   2746.8

7) Mr. Jansen is building an ice rink in his backyard that will measure 8.4 meters by 22 meters. What is the area of the rink?

84 tenths
22
168
168   184.8 sq. meters
1848 Tenths

8) Rachel runs 3.2 miles each week day and 1.5 each day of the weekend. How many miles will she run in 6 weeks?

32
5
160 tenths

15
2
30 tenths

16
3
19 miles

19
6
114 miles

9) A slice of pizza costs $1.57. How much does 27 slices cost?

157
27
999
314   4039 cents $40.39

10) A spool of ribbon holds 6.75 meters. If the craft club buys 21 spools what is the total cost of the ribbon selling for $2 per meter.

675
21
675
1350
14175 h

141.75
2
28350 h $283.60

CPSIA information can be obtained
at www.ICGtesting.com
Printed in the USA
LVOW02s0014240816

501544LV00005BA/20/P

9 781631 897955